Marx
Defoe Abbott Hardy Melville Montaigne Machiavelli Haggard esterton ooper erson Austen Hugo Grimm Eliot
Stoker Carroll Christie Molière
Wilde Maupassant Byron Schiller
Garnett Fitzgerald Einstein Engels Smith Kafka
Goethe Hawthorne Hall
Cotton Dostoyevsky
Baum Kipling Doyle Willis
Leslie Dumas Henry Nietzsche
Flaubert Turgenev Balzac
Stockton Vatsyayana Crane
Burroughs Verne
Curtis Tocqueville Gogol Vinci
Homer Widger Whitman Busch
Darwin Tolstoy
Potter Freud Thoreau Twain Scott Harte
Kant Zola Lawrence Plato
Jowett Stevenson Dickens Burton Hesse
Andersen
London Descartes Voltaire Cervantes
Poe Aristotle Wells
Hale James Hastings Cooke
Bunner Shakespeare Irving
Richter Chambers da
Doré Chekhov Benedict Alcott
Dante Shaw Pushkin
Swift Wodehouse Newton

⊕ tredition®

tredition was established in 2006 by Sandra Latusseck and Soenke Schulz. Based in Hamburg, Germany, tredition offers publishing solutions to authors and publishing houses, combined with world-wide distribution of printed and digital book content. tredition is uniquely positioned to enable authors and publishing houses to create books on their own terms and without conventional manu-facturing risks.

For more information please visit: www.tredition.com

TREDITION CLASSICS

This book is part of the TREDITION CLASSICS series. The creators of this series are united by passion for literature and driven by the intention of making all public domain books available in printed format again - worldwide. Most TREDITION CLASSICS titles have been out of print and off the bookstore shelves for decades. At tredi-tion we believe that a great book never goes out of style and that its value is eternal. Several mostly non-profit literature projects pro-vide content to tredition. To support their good work, tredition donates a portion of the proceeds from each sold copy. As a reader of a TREDITION CLASSICS book, you support our mission to save many of the amazing works of world literature from oblivion. See all available books at www.tredition.com.

⊘ Project Gutenberg

The content for this book has been graciously provided by Project Gutenberg. Project Gutenberg is a non-profit organization founded by Michael Hart in 1971 at the University of Illinois. The mission of Project Gutenberg is simple: To encourage the creation and distribu-tion of eBooks. Project Gutenberg is the first and largest collection of public domain eBooks.

Richard I Makers of History

Jacob Abbott

Imprint

This book is part of TREDITION CLASSICS

Author: Jacob Abbott
Cover design: Buchgut, Berlin – Germany

Publisher: tredition GmbH, Hamburg - Germany
ISBN: 978-3-8472-2096-1

www.tredition.com
www.tredition.de

Makers of History

Richard I.

By JACOB ABBOTT

WITH ENGRAVINGS

NEW YORK AND LONDON

HARPER & BROTHERS PUBLISHERS

1902

PREFACE.

The author of this series has made it his special object to confine himself very strictly, even in the most minute details which he records, to historic truth. The narratives are not tales founded upon history, but history itself, without any embellishment, or any deviations from the strict truth so far as it can now be discovered by an attentive examination of the annals written at the time when the events themselves occurred. In writing the narratives, the author has endeavored to avail himself of the best sources of information which this country affords; and though, of course, there must be in these volumes, as in all historical accounts, more or less of imperfection and error, there is no intentional embellishment. Nothing is stated, not even the most minute and apparently imaginary details, without what was deemed good historical authority. The readers, therefore, may rely upon the record as the truth, and nothing but the truth, so far as an honest purpose and a careful examination have been effectual in ascertaining it.

KING RICHARD I.

Chapter I.

King Richard's Mother.

1137-1154

Richard the Crusader.
A quarrelsome king.

King Richard the First, the Crusader, was a boisterous, reckless, and desperate man, and he made a great deal of noise in the world in his day. He began his career very early in life by quarreling with his father. Indeed, his father, his mother, and all his brothers and sisters were engaged, as long as the father lived, in perpetual wars against each other, which were waged with the most desperate fierceness on all sides. The subject of these quarrels was the different possessions which the various branches of the family held or claimed in France and in England, each endeavoring to dispossess the others. In order to understand the nature of these difficulties, and also to comprehend fully what sort of a woman Richard's mother was, we must first pay a little attention [Pg 14] to the map of the countries over which these royal personages held sway.

Richard's kingdom.
Union of England and Normandy.
England was a possession of Normandy.

We have already seen, in another volume of this series, [A] how
the two countries of Normandy on the Continent, and of England,
became united under one government. England, however, did [Pg
15] not conquer and hold Normandy; it was Normandy that conquered and held England. The relative situation of these two countries is shown on the map. Normandy, it will be seen, was situated
in the northern part of France, being separated from England by the
English Channel. Besides Normandy, the sovereigns of the country
held various other possessions in France, and this French portion of
the compound realm over which they reigned they considered as
far the most important portion. England was but a sort of append-
age to their empire.

Eleanora of Aquitaine.

You will see by the map the situation of the River Loire. It rises in the centre of France, and flows to the westward, through a country which was, even in those days, very fertile and beautiful. South of the Loire was a sort of kingdom, then under the dominion of a young and beautiful princess named Eleanora. The name of her kingdom was Aquitaine. This lady afterward became the mother of Richard. She was very celebrated in her day, and has since been greatly renowned in history under the name of Eleanora of Aquitaine.

The contemporaries of Eleanora.
Royal match-making.

Eleanora received her realm from her grandfather. Her father had gone on a crusade with his brother, Eleanora's uncle, Raymond, and had [Pg 16] been killed in the East. Raymond had made himself master of Antioch. We shall presently hear of this Raymond again. The grandfather abdicated in Eleanora's favor when she was about fourteen years of age. There were two other powerful sovereigns in France at this time, Louis, King of France, who reigned in Paris, and Henry, Duke of Normandy and King of England. King Louis of France had a son, the Prince Louis, who was heir to the crown. Eleanora's grandfather formed the scheme of marrying her to this Prince Louis, and thus to unite his kingdom to hers. He himself was tired of ruling, and wished to resign his power, with a view of spending the rest of his days in penitence and prayer. He had been a very wicked man in his day, and now, as he was growing old, he was harassed by remorse for his sins, and wished, if possible, to make some atonement for them by his penances before he died.

The conditions of the marriage.

So he called all his barons together, and laid his plans before them. They consented to them on two conditions. One was, that Eleanora should first see Louis, and say whether she was willing to have him for her husband. If not, she was not to be compelled to marry him. The other condition was, that their country, [Pg 17] Aquitaine, was not to be combined with the dominions of the King of France after the marriage, but was to continue a separate and independent realm, to be governed by Louis and Eleanora, not as King and Queen of France, but as Duke and Duchess of Aquitaine.

Both these conditions were complied with. The interview was arranged between Louis and Eleanora, and Eleanora concluded that she should like the king for a husband very much. At least she said so, and the marriage was concluded.

Apparent prosperity of Eleanora.

Indeed, the match thus arranged for Eleanora was, in all worldly respects, the most eligible one that could be made. Her husband was the heir-apparent to the throne of France. His capital was Paris, which was then, as now, the great centre in Europe of all splendor and gayety. The father of Louis was old, and not likely to live long; indeed, he died very soon after the marriage, and thus Eleanora, when scarcely fifteen, became Queen of France as well as Duchess of Aquitaine, and was thus raised to the highest pinnacle of worldly grandeur.

Eleanora's accomplishments.

She was young and beautiful, and very gay in her disposition, and she entered at once upon a life of pleasure. She had been well educated. She could sing the songs of the Troubadours, [Pg 18] which was the fashionable music of those days, in a most charming manner. Indeed, she composed music herself, and wrote lines to accompany it. She was quite celebrated for her learning, on account of her being able both to read and write: these were rare accomplishments for ladies in those days.

The Crusades.

She spent a considerable portion of her time in Paris, at the court of her husband, but then she often returned to Aquitaine, where she held a sort of court of her own in Bordeaux, which was her capital. She led this sort of life for some time, until at length she was induced to form a design of going to the East on a crusade. The Crusades were military expeditions which went from the western countries of Europe to conquer Palestine from the Turks, in order to recover possession of Jerusalem and of the sepulchre where the body of Christ was laid.

A monk preaching the Crusades.

It had been for some time the practice for the princes and knights, and other potentates of France and England, to go on these expeditions, on account of the fame and glory which those who distinguished themselves acquired. The people were excited, moreover, to join the Crusades by the preachings of monks and hermits, who harangued them in public places and [Pg 19] urged them to go. At these assemblages the monks held up symbols of the crucifixion, to inspire their zeal, and promised them the special favor of heaven if they would go. They said that whoever devoted himself to this great cause should surely be pardoned for all the sins and crimes that he had committed, whatever they might be; and whenever they heard of the commission of any great crimes by potentates or rulers, they would seize upon the occasion to urge the guilty persons to go and fight for the cross in Palestine, as a means of wiping away their guilt.

PREACHING THE CRUSADES.
The reasons why Louis and Eleanora undertook a crusade.

One of these preachers charged such a crime [Pg 20] upon Louis, the husband of Eleanora. It seems that, in a quarrel which he had with one of his neighbors, he had sent an armed force to invade his enemy's dominions, and in storming a town a cathedral had been set on fire and burned, and fifteen hundred persons, who had taken refuge in it as a sanctuary, had perished in the flames. Now it was a very great crime, according to the ideas of those times, to violate a sanctuary; and the hermit-preacher urged Louis to go on a crusade in order to atone for the dreadful guilt he had incurred by not only violating a sanctuary, but by overwhelming, in doing it, so many hundreds of innocent women and children in the awful suffering of being burned to death. So Louis determined to go on a crusade, and Eleanora determined to accompany him. Her motive was a love of adventure and a fondness for notoriety. She thought that by going out, a young and beautiful princess, at the head of an army of Crusaders, into the East, she would make herself a renowned heroine in the eyes of the whole world. So she immediately commenced her preparations, and by the commanding influence which she exerted over the ladies of the court, she soon inspired them all with her own romantic ardor.

[Pg 21]

Amazons.
The power of ridicule.

The ladies at once laid aside their feminine dress, and clothed themselves like Amazons, so that they could ride astride on horseback like men. All their talk was of arms, and armor, and horses, and camps. They endeavored, too, to interest all the men—the princes, and barons, and knights that surrounded them—in their plans, and to induce them to join the expedition. A great many did so, but there were some that shook their heads and seemed inclined to stay at home. They knew that so wild and heedless a plan as this could end in nothing but disaster. The ladies ridiculed these men for their cowardice and want of spirit, and they sent them their distaffs as presents. "We have no longer any use for the distaffs," said they, "but, as you are intending to stay at home and make women of yourselves, we send them to you, so that you may occupy yourselves with spinning while we are gone." By such taunts and ridicule as this, a great many were shamed into joining the expedition, whose good sense made them extremely averse to have any thing to do with it.

The plans and purposes of the female Crusaders.

The expedition was at length organized and prepared to set forth. It was encumbered by the immense quantity of baggage which the [Pg 22] queen and her party of women insisted on taking. It is true that they had assumed the dress of Amazons, but this was only for the camp and the field. They expected to enjoy a great many pleasures while they were gone, to give and receive a great many entertainments, and to live in luxury and splendor in the great cities of the East. So they must needs take with them large quantities of baggage, containing dresses and stores of female paraphernalia of all kinds. The king remonstrated against this folly, but all to no purpose. The ladies thought it very hard if, in going on such an expedition, they could not take with them the usual little comforts and conveniences appropriate to their sex. So it ended with their having their own way.

Antioch.
Meeting the Saracens.

The caprices and freaks of these women continued to harass and interfere with the expedition during the whole course of it. The army of Crusaders reached at length a place near Antioch, in Asia Minor, where they encountered the Saracens. Antioch was then in the possession of the Christians. It was under the command of the Prince Raymond, who has already been spoken of as Eleanora's uncle. Raymond was a young and very handsome prince, and Eleanora anticipated great pleasure in visiting [Pg 23] his capital. The expedition had not, however, yet reached it, but were advancing through the country, defending themselves as well as they could against the troops of Arab horsemen that were harassing their march.

Choosing an encampment.
The result of the queen's generalship.

The commanders were greatly perplexed in this emergency to know what to do with the women, and with their immense train of baggage. The king at last sent them on in advance, with all his best troops to accompany them. He directed them to go on, and encamp for the night on certain high ground which he designated, where they would be safe, he said, from an attack by the Arabs. But when they approached the place, Eleanora found a green and fertile valley near, which was very romantic and beautiful, and she decided at once that this was a much prettier place to encamp in than the bare hill above. The officers in command of the troops remonstrated in vain. Eleanora and the ladies insisted on encamping in the valley. The consequence was, that the Arabs came and got possession of the hill, and thus put themselves between the division of the army which was with Eleanora and that which was advancing under the king. A great battle was fought. The French were defeated. A [Pg 24] great many thousand men were slain. All the provisions for the army were cut off, and all the ladies' baggage was seized and plundered by the Arabs. The remainder of the army, with the king, and the queen, and the ladies, succeeded in making their escape to Antioch, and there Prince Raymond opened the gates and let them in.

A quarrel.

As soon as Eleanora and the other ladies recovered a little from their fright and fatigue, they began to lead very gay lives in Antioch, and before long a serious quarrel broke out between Louis and the queen. The cause of this quarrel was Raymond. He was a young and handsome man, and he soon began to show such fondness for Eleanora that the king's jealousy was aroused, and at length the king discerned, as he said, proofs of such a degree of intimacy between them as to fill him with rage. He determined to leave Antioch immediately, and take Eleanora with him. She was very unwilling to go, but the king was so angry that he compelled her to accompany him. So he went away abruptly, scarcely bidding Raymond good-by at all, and proceeded with Eleanora and nearly all his company to Jerusalem. Eleanora submitted, though she was exceedingly out of humor.

[Pg 25]

The queen at Jerusalem.
A divorce proposed.

The king, too, on his part, was as much out of humor as the queen. He determined that he would not allow her to accompany him any more on the campaign; so he left her at Jerusalem, a sort of prisoner, while he put himself at the head of his army and went forth to prosecute the war. By-and-by, when he came back to Jerusalem, and inquired about his wife's conduct while he had been gone, he learned some facts in respect to the intimacy which she had formed with a prince of the country during his absence, that made him more angry than ever. He declared that he would sue for a divorce. She was a wicked woman, he said, and he would repudiate her.

One of his ministers, however, contrived to appease him, at least so far as to induce him to abandon this design. The minister did not pretend to say that Eleanora was innocent, or that she did not deserve to be repudiated, but he said that if the divorce was to be carried into effect, then Louis would lose all claim to Eleanora's possessions, for it will be recollected that the dukedom of Aquitaine, and the other rich possessions which belonged to Eleanora before her marriage, continued entirely separate from the kingdom of France, and still belonged to her.

[Pg 26]

The king and Eleanora had a daughter named Margaret, who was now a young child, but who, when she grew up, would inherit both her father's and her mother's possessions, and thus, in the end, they would be united, if the king and queen continued to live together in peace. But this would be all lost, as the minister maintained in his argument with the king, in case of a divorce.

"If you are divorced from her," said he, "she will soon be married again, and then all her possessions will finally go out of your family."

The failure of the crusade.
Returning to France.

So the king concluded to submit to the shame of his wife's dishonor, and still keep her as his wife. But he had now lost all interest in the crusade, partly on account of his want of success in it, and partly on account of his domestic troubles. So he left the Holy Land, and took the queen and the ladies, and the remnant of his troops, back again to Paris. Here he and the queen lived very unhappily together for about two years.

The queen's new lover.
A divorce again proposed.

At the end of this time the queen became involved in new difficulties in consequence of her intrigues. The time had passed away so rapidly that it was now thirteen years since her marriage, [Pg 27] and she was about twenty-eight years of age—old enough, one would think, to have learned some discretion. After, however, amusing herself with various lovers, she at length became enamored of a young prince named Henry Plantagenet, who afterward became Henry the Second of England, and was the father of Richard, the hero of this history. Henry was at this time Duke of Normandy. He came to visit the court of Louis in Paris, and here, after a short time, Eleanora conceived the idea of being divorced from Louis in order to marry him. Henry was a great deal younger than Eleanora, being then only about eighteen years of age; but he was very agreeable in his person and manners, and Queen Eleanora was quite charmed with him. It was not, however, to be expected that he should be so much charmed with her; for, although she had been very beautiful, she had now so far passed the period of her youth, and had been subjected to so many exposures, that the bloom of her early beauty was in a great measure gone. She was now nearly thirty years old, having been married twelve or thirteen years. She, however, made eager advances to Henry, and finally gave him to understand, that if he would consent to [Pg 28] marry her, she would obtain a divorce from King Louis, and then endow him with all her dominions.

The motives of Henry.

Now there was a strong reason operating upon Henry's mind to accept this proposal. He claimed to be entitled to the crown of England. King Stephen was at this time reigning in England, but Henry maintained that he was a usurper, and he was eager to dispossess him. Eleanora represented to Henry that, with all the forces of her dominions, she could easily enable him to do that, and so at length the idea of making himself a king overcame his natural repugnance to take a wife almost twice as old as he was himself, and she, too, the divorced and discarded wife of another man. So he agreed to Eleanora's proposal, and measures were soon taken to effect the divorce.

Controversy among historians.
The real motives in the divorce.

There is some dispute among the ancient historians in respect to this divorce. Some say that it was the king that originated it, and that the cause which he alleged was the freedom of the queen in her love for other men, and that Eleanora, when she found that the divorce was resolved upon, formed the plan of beguiling young Henry into a marriage with her, to save her fall. Others say that the divorce was her [Pg 29] plan alone, and that the pretext for it was the relationship that existed between her and King Louis, for they were in some degree related to each other; and the rules of the Church of Rome were very strict against such marriages. It is not improbable, however, that the real reason of the divorce was that the king desired it on account of his wife's loose and irregular character, while Eleanora wished for it in order to have a more agreeable husband. She never had liked Louis. He was a very grave and even gloomy man, who thought of nothing but the Church, and his penances and prayers, so that Eleanora said he was more of a monk than a king. This monkish turn of mind had increased upon the king since his return from the Crusades. He made it a matter of conscience to wear coarse and plain clothes instead of dressing handsomely like a king, and he cut off the curls of his hair, which had been very beautiful, and shaved his head and his mustaches. This procedure disgusted Eleanora completely. She despised her husband herself, and ridiculed him to others, saying that he had made himself look like an old priest. In a word, all her love for him was entirely gone. Both parties being thus very willing to have the marriage annulled, [Pg 30] they agreed to put it on the ground of their relationship, in order to avoid scandal.

A violent courtship and a narrow escape.

At any rate, the marriage was dissolved, and Eleanora set out from Paris to return to Bordeaux, the capital of her own country. Henry was to meet her on the way. Her road lay along the banks of the Loire. Here she stopped for a day or two. The count who ruled this province, who was a very gay and handsome man, offered her his hand. He wished to add her dominions to his own. Eleanora refused him. The count resolved not to take the refusal, and, under some pretext or other, he detained her in his castle, resolving to keep her there until she should consent. But Eleanora was not a woman to be conquered by such a method as this. She pretended to acquiesce in the detention, and to be contented, but this was only to put the count off his guard; and then, watching her opportunity, she escaped from the castle in the night; and getting into a boat, which she had caused to be provided for the purpose, she went down the river to the town of Tours, which was some distance below, and in the dominions of another sovereign.

Geoffrey's designs upon Eleanora.
Customs of old times.

In going on from Tours toward her own home, she encountered and narrowly escaped another [Pg 31] danger. It seems that Geoffrey Plantagenet, the brother of Henry, whom she had engaged to marry, conceived the design of seizing her and compelling her to marry him instead of his brother. It may seem strange that any one should be so unprincipled and base as to attempt thus to circumvent his own brother, and take away from him his intended wife; but it was not a strange thing at all for the members of the royal and princely families of those days to act in this manner toward each other. It was the usual and established condition of things among these families that the different members of them should be perpetually intriguing and manœuvring one against the other, brother against sister, husband against wife, and father against son. In a vast number of instances these contentions broke out into open war, and the wars thus waged between the nearest relatives were of the most desperate and merciless character.

Eleanora eluded Geoffrey.

It was therefore a very moderate and inconsiderable deed of brotherly hostility on the part of Geoffrey to plan the seizure of his brother's intended wife, in order to get possession of her dominions. The plan which he formed was to lie in wait for the boat which was to convey Eleanora down the river, and seize her as she [Pg 32] came by. She, however, avoided this snare by turning off into a branch of the river which came from the south. You will see the course of the river and the situation of this southern branch on the map. [B] The branch which Eleanora followed not only took her away from the ambush which Geoffrey had laid for her, but conducted her toward her own home, where, after meeting with various other adventures, she arrived safely at last. Here Henry Plantagenet soon joined her, and they were married. The marriage took place only six weeks after her divorce from her former husband. This was considered a very scandalous transaction throughout, and Eleanora was now considered as having forfeited all claims to respectability of character. Still she was a great duchess in her own right, and was now wife of the heir-apparent of the English throne, and so her character made little difference in the estimation in which she was held by the world.

She is married to Henry.

From the time of her first engagement with Henry nearly two years had elapsed before all the proceedings in relation to the divorce had been completed so as to prepare the way for the marriage, and now Eleanora was about thirty-two [Pg 33] years of age, while Henry was only twenty. Henry seems to have felt no love for his wife. He had acceded to her proposal to marry him only in order to obtain the assistance which the forces of her dominions might supply him in gaining possession of the English throne.

Henry's expedition to England.
His final coronation.

Accordingly, about a year after the marriage, a military expedition was fitted out to proceed to England. The expedition consisted of thirty-six ships, and a large force of fighting men. Henry landed in England at the head of this force, and advanced against Stephen. The two princes fought for some time without any very decisive success on either side, when at length they concluded to settle the quarrel by a compromise. It was agreed that Stephen should continue to hold the crown as long as he lived, and then that Henry should succeed him. When this arrangement had been made, Henry returned to Normandy; and then, after two or three years, he heard of Stephen's death. He then went immediately to England again, and was universally acknowledged as king. Eleanora went with him as queen, and very soon they were crowned at Westminster with the greatest possible pomp and parade.

[Pg 34]

Eleanora Queen of England.

And thus it was that Eleanora of Aquitaine, the mother of Richard, in the year eleven hundred and fifty-four, became queen-consort of England.

[Pg 35]

Chapter II.

Richard's early Life.

1154-1184

The sons and daughters of King Henry.
Rebellions and family quarrels.

Almost all the early years of the life of our hero were spent in wars which were waged by the different members of his father's family against each other. These wars originated in the quarrels that arose between the sons and their father in respect to the family property and power. Henry had five sons, of whom Richard was the third. He had also three daughters. The king held a great variety of possessions, having inherited from his father and grandfather, or received through his wife, a number of distinct and independent realms. Thus he was duke of one country, earl of another, king of a third, and count of a fourth. England was his kingdom, Normandy was his great dukedom, and he held, besides, various other realms. He was a generous father, and he began early by conveying some of these provinces to his sons. But they were not contented with the portions that he voluntarily assigned them. [Pg 36] They called for more. Sometimes the father yielded to these unreasonable demands, but yielding only made the young men more grasping than before, and at length the father would resist. Then came rebellions, and leagues formed by the sons against the father, and the musterings of armies, and battles, and sieges. The mother generally took part with the sons in these unnatural contests, and in the course of them the most revolting spectacles were presented to the eyes of the world—of towns belonging to a father sacked and burned by the sons, or castles beleaguered, and the garrisons reduced to famine, in which a husband was defending himself against the forces of his wife, or a sister against those of a brother. Richard himself, who seems to have been the most desperate and reckless of the family, began to take an active part in these rebellions against his father when he was only seventeen years old.

These wars continued, with various temporary interruptions, for many years, and whenever at any time a brief peace was made between the sons and the father, then the young men would usually fall to quarreling among themselves. Indeed, Henry, the oldest of them, said that the only possible bond of peace between [Pg 37] the brothers seemed to be a common war against their father.

The appearance of the Queen Eleanora in London.

Nor did the king live on much better terms with his wife than he did with his children. At the time of Eleanora's marriage with Henry, her prospects were bright indeed. The people of England, notwithstanding the evil reports that were spread in respect to her character, received her as their queen with much enthusiasm, and on the occasion of her coronation they made a great deal of parade to celebrate the event. Her appearance at that time attracted unusual attention. This was partly on account of her personal attractions and partly on account of her dress. The style of her dress was quite Oriental. She had brought home with her from Antioch a great many Eastern fashions, and many elegant articles of dress, such as mantles of silk and brocade, scarfs, jeweled girdles and bands, and beautiful veils, such as are worn at the East. These dresses were made at Constantinople, and when displayed by the queen in London they received a great deal of admiration.

Illuminated portraits.
The queen's attire.

We can see precisely how the queen looked in these dresses by means of illuminated portraits of her contained in the books written at [Pg 38] that time. It was the custom in those days in writing books — the work of which was all executed by hand — to embellish them with what were called illuminations. These were small paintings inserted here and there upon the page, representing the distinguished personages named in the writing. These portraits were painted in very brilliant colors, and there are several still remaining that show precisely how Eleanora appeared in one of her Oriental dresses. She wears a close head-dress, with a circlet of gems over it. There is a gown made with tight sleeves, and fastened with full gathers just below the throat, where it is confined by a rich collar of gems. Over this is an elegant outer robe bordered with fur. The sleeves of the outer robe are very full and loose, and are lined with ermine. They open so as to show the close sleeves beneath. Over all is a long and beautiful gauze veil.

The king's attire.

The dress of the king was very rich and gorgeous too; and so, indeed, was that of all the ecclesiastics and other dignitaries that took part in the celebration. All London was filled with festivity and rejoicing on the occasion, and the queen's heart overflowed with pride and joy.

The palace at Bermondsey.
Scenes of festivity.

After the coronation, the king conducted Eleanora [Pg 39] to a beautiful country residence called Bermondsey, which was at a short distance from London, toward the south. Here there was a palace, and gardens, and beautiful grounds. The palace was on an elevation which commanded a fine view of the capital. Here the queen lived in royal state. She had, however, other palaces besides, and she often went to and fro among her different residences. She contrived a great many entertainments to amuse her court, such as comedies, games, revels, and celebrations of all sorts. The king joined with her in these schemes of pleasure. One of the historians of the time gives a curious account of the appearance of the king and the court in their excursions. "When the king sets out of a morning, you see multitudes of people running up and down as if they were distracted—horses rushing against horses, carriages overturning carriages, players, gamesters, cooks, confectioners, morrice-dancers, barbers, courtezans, and parasites—making so much noise, and, in a word, such an intolerable tumultuous jumble of horse and foot, that you can imagine the great abyss hath opened and poured forth all its inhabitants."

The palace at Oxford.
Its present appearance.

It was about three years after Eleanora was [Pg 40] crowned Queen of England that Richard was born. At the time of his birth, the queen was residing at a palace in Oxford. The palace has gone pretty much to ruin. The building is now used in part as a work-house. The room where Richard was born is roofless and uninhabitable. Nothing even of the interior of it remains except some traces of the fire-place. The room, however, though thus completely gone to ruin, is a place of considerable interest to the English people, who visit it in great numbers in order that they may see the place where the great hero was born; for, desperate and reckless as Richard's character was, the people of England are quite proud of him on account of his undaunted bravery.

An early marriage.
The reason for marrying children four years old.

It is very curious that the first important event of Richard's child-hood was his marriage. He was married when he was about four years old—that is, he was regularly and formally affianced, and a ceremony which might be called the marriage ceremony was duly performed. His bride was a young child of Louis, King of France. The child was about three years old. Her name was Alice. This marriage was the result of a sort of bargain between Henry, Richard's father, and Louis, the French king. They [Pg 41] had had a fierce dispute about the portion of another of Louis's children that had been married in the same way to one of Richard's brothers named Henry. The English king complained that the dowry was not sufficient, and the French king, after a long discussion, agreed to make it up by giving another province with his daughter Alice to Richard. The reason that induced the King of England to effect these marriages was, that the provinces that were bestowed with their infant wives as their dowries came into his hands as the guardian of their husbands while they were minors, and thus extended, as it were, his own dominions.

Vice-regencies.
The rebellions of Richard.

By this time the realms of King Henry had become very extensive. He inherited Normandy, you will recollect, from his ancestors, and he was in possession of that country before he became King of England. When he was married to Eleanora, he acquired through her a large addition to his territory by becoming, jointly with her, the sovereign of her realms in the south of France. Then, when he became King of England, his power was still more extended, and, finally, by the marriages of his sons, the young princes, he received other provinces besides, though, of course, he held these [Pg 42] last only as the guardian of his children. Now, in governing these various realms, the king was accustomed to leave his wife and his sons in different portions of them, to rule them in his absence, though still under his command. They each maintained a sort of court in the city where their father left them, but they were expected to govern the several portions of the country in strict subjection to their father's general control. The boys, however, as they grew older, became more and more independent in feeling; and the queen, being a great deal older than her husband, and having been, before her marriage, a sovereign in her own right, was disposed to be very little submissive to his authority. It was under these circumstances that the family quarrels arose that led to the wars spoken of at the beginning of the chapter. Richard himself, as was there stated, began to raise rebellions against his father when he was about seventeen years old.

Whenever, in the course of these wars, the young men found themselves worsted in their contests with their father's troops, their resource was to fly to Paris, in order to get King Louis to aid them. This Louis was always willing to do, for he took great pleasure in the dissensions [Pg 43] which were thus continually breaking out in Henry's family.

Eleanora's time of suffering comes.
The queen's flight.

Besides these wars, Queen Eleanora had one great and bitter source of trouble in a guilty attachment which her husband cherished for a beautiful lady more nearly of his own age than his wife was. Her name was Rosamond. She is known in history as Fair Rosamond. A full account of her will be given in the next chapter. All that is necessary to state here is that Queen Eleanora was made very wretched by her husband's love for Rosamond, though she had scarcely any right to complain, for she had, as it would seem, done all in her power to alienate the affections of her husband from herself by the levity of her conduct, and by her bold and independent behavior in all respects. At last, at one time while she was at Bordeaux, the capital of her realm of Aquitaine, she heard rumors that the king was intending to obtain a divorce from her, in order that he might openly marry Rosamond, and she determined to go back to her former husband, Louis of France. The country, however, was full of castles, which were garrisoned by Henry's troops, and she was afraid that they would prevent her going if they knew of her intention; so she contrived a plan [Pg 44] of disguising herself in man's clothes, and undertook to make her escape in that way. She succeeded in getting away from Bordeaux, but her flight was soon discovered, and the officers of the garrison immediately sent off a party to pursue her. The pursuers overtook her before she had gone far, and brought her back. They treated her quite roughly, and kept her a prisoner in Bordeaux until her husband came. When Henry arrived he was quite angry with the queen for having thus undertaken to go back to her former husband, whom he considered as his greatest rival and enemy, and he determined that she should have no opportunity to make another such attempt; so he kept a very strict watch over her, and subjected her to so much restraint that she considered herself a prisoner.

The captivity in Winchester.

The king had a quarrel also at this time with one of his daughters-in-law, and he made her a prisoner too. Soon after this he went back to England, taking these two captives in his train. In a short time he sent the queen to a certain palace which he had in Winchester, and there he kept her confined for sixteen years. It was during this period of their mother's captivity that the wars between the father and his sons was waged most fiercely.

[Pg 45]

The message from Henry.
His death.

At length, in the year eleven hundred and eighty-two, in the midst of one of the most violent wars that had raged between the king and his sons, a message came to the king that his son Henry was very dangerously sick, and that he wished his father to come and see him. The king was greatly at a loss what to do on receiving this communication. His counselors advised him not to go. It was only a stratagem, they said, on the part of the young prince, to get his father into his camp, and so take him prisoner. So the king concluded not to go. He had, however, some misgivings that his son might be really sick, and accordingly dispatched an archbishop to him with a ring, which he said he sent to him as a token of his forgiveness and of his paternal affection. Very soon, however, a second messenger came to the king to say that Prince Henry had died. These sad tidings overwhelmed the heart of the king with the most poignant grief. He at once forgot all the undutiful and disobedient conduct of his son, and remembered him only as his dearly-beloved child. He became almost broken-hearted.

Remorse.
The agonies of a wicked man's death.

The prince himself, on his death-bed, was borne down with remorse and anguish in thinking of the crimes that he had committed against [Pg 46] his father. He longed to have his father come and see him before he died. The ring which the archbishop was sent to bring to him arrived just in time, and the prince pressed it to his lips, and blessed it with tears of frantic grief. As the hour of death approached his remorse became dreadful. All the attempts made by the priests around his bed to soothe and quiet him were unavailing, and at last his agony became so great that he compelled them to put a rope around him and drag him from his bed to a heap of ashes, placed for the purpose in his room, that he might die there. A heap of ashes, he said, was the only fit place for such a reprobate as he had been.

So will it be with all undutiful children; when on their death-beds, they reflect on their disobedient and rebellious conduct toward the father and the mother to whom they owe their being.

Affliction reconciles hostile relatives.

It is remarkable how great an effect a death in a family produces in reconciling those who before had been at enmity with each other. There are many husbands and wives who greatly disagree with each other in times of health and prosperity, but who are reconciled and made to love each other by adversity and sorrow. [Pg 47] Such was the effect produced upon the minds of Henry and Eleanora by the death of their son and heir. They were both overwhelmed with grief, for the affection which a parent bears to a child is never wholly extinguished, however undutiful and rebellious a child may be; and the grief which the two parents now felt in common brought them to a reconciliation. The king seemed disposed to forgive the queen for the offenses, whether real or imaginary, which she had committed against him. "Now that our dear son is dead and gone," said he, "let us no longer quarrel with each other." So he liberated the queen from the restraint which he had imposed upon her, and restored her once more to her rank as an English queen.

Another quarrel.

This state of things continued for about a year, and then the old spirit of animosity and contention burned up once more as fiercely as ever. The king shut up Eleanora again, and a violent quarrel broke out between the king and his son Richard.

Richard's long engagement.

The cause of this quarrel was connected with the Princess Alice, to whom it will be recollected Richard had been betrothed in his infancy. Richard claimed that now, since he was of age, his wife ought to be given to him, but his father [Pg 48] kept her away, and would not allow the marriage to be consummated. The king made various excuses and pretexts for the delay. Some thought that the real reason was that he wished to continue his guardianship and his possession of the dower as long as possible, but Richard thought that his father was in love with Alice himself, and that he did not intend that he, Richard, should have her at all. This difficulty led to new quarrels, in which the king and Richard became more exasperated with each other than ever. This state of things continued until Richard was thirty-four years old and his bride was thirty. Richard was so far bound to her that he could not marry any other lady, and his father obstinately persisted in preventing his completing the marriage with her.

[Pg 49]

Portrait of King Henry II.

PORTRAIT OF
KING HENRY II.
The sad death of Geoffrey.
Dividing the inheritance.

In the mean time Prince Geoffrey, another of the king's sons, came to a miserable end. He was killed in a tournament. He was riding furiously in the tournament in the midst of a great number of other horsemen, when he was unfortunately thrown from his steed, and trodden to death on the ground by the hoofs of the other horses that galloped over him. The only two sons that were now left were Richard and John. Of these, Richard was now the oldest, and he was, of course, his father's heir. King Henry, however, formed a plan for dividing his dominions between his two sons, instead of allowing Richard to inherit the whole. John was his youngest son, and, as such, the king loved him tenderly. So he conceived the idea of [Pg 50] leaving to Richard all his possessions in France, which constituted the most important part of his dominions, and of bestowing the kingdom of England upon John; and, in order to make sure of the carrying of this arrangement into effect, he proposed crowning John king of England forthwith.

Richard's resistance to his father's plans.

Richard, however, determined to resist this plan. The former king of France, Louis the Seventh, was now dead, and his son, Philip the Second, the brother of Alice, reigned in his stead. Richard immediately set off for Paris, and laid his case before the young French king. "I am engaged," said he, "to your sister Alice, and my father will not give her to me. Help me to maintain my rights and hers."

Assistance from Philip.
King Henry's reproach of his son John.

Philip, like his father, was always ready to do any thing in his power to foment dissensions in the family of Henry. So he readily took Richard's part in this new quarrel, and he, somehow or other, contrived means to induce John to come and join in the rebellion. King Henry was overwhelmed with grief when he learned that John, his youngest, and now his dearest child, and the last that remained, had abandoned him. His grief was mingled with resentment and rage. He invoked the bitterest [Pg 51] curses on his children's heads, and he caused a device to be painted for John and sent to him, representing a young eaglet picking out the parent eagle's eyes. This was to typify to him his own undutiful and unnatural behavior.

Lady Rosamond.

Thus the domestic life which Richard led while he was a young man was imbittered by the continual quarrels between the father, the mother, and the children. The greatest source of sorrow to his mother, however, was the connection which subsisted between the king and the Lady Rosamond. The nature and the results of this connection will be explained in the next chapter.

[Pg 52]

Chapter III.

Fair Rosamond.

1184

The mystery surrounding Fair Rosamond's history.

During his lifetime King Henry did every thing in his power, of course, to keep the circumstances of his connection with Rosamond a profound secret, and to mislead people as much as possible in regard to her. After his death, too, it was for the interest of his family that as little as possible should be known respecting her. Thus it happened that, in the absence of all authentic information, a great many strange rumors and legends were put in circulation, and at length, when the history of those times came to be written, it was impossible to separate the false from the true.

The valley of the Wye.

The truth, however, so far as it can now be ascertained, seems to be something like this: Rosamond was the daughter of an English nobleman named Clifford. Lord Clifford lived in a fine old castle situated in the valley of the Wye, in a most romantic and beautiful situation. The River Wye is in the western part of England. It flows out from among the [Pg 53] mountains of Wales through a wild and romantic gorge, which, after passing the English frontier, expands into a broad, and fertile, and most beautiful valley. The castle of Lord Clifford was built at the opening of the gorge, and it commanded an enchanting view of the valley below.

The clandestine marriage.

It was here that Rosamond spent her childhood, and here probably that Henry first met her while he was yet a young man. She was extremely beautiful, and Henry fell very deeply in love with her. This was while they were both very young, and some time before Henry thought of Eleanora for his wife. There is some reason to believe that Henry was really married to Rosamond, though, if so, the marriage was a private one, and the existence of it was kept a profound secret from all the world. The real and public marriages of kings and princes are almost always determined by reasons of state; and when Henry at last went to Paris, and saw Eleanora there, and found, moreover, that she was willing to marry him, and to bring him as her dowry all her possessions in France, which would so greatly extend his dominions, he determined to accede to her desires, and to keep his connection with Rosamond, [Pg 54] whatever the nature of it might have been, a profound secret forever.

So he married Eleanora and brought her to England, and lived with her, as has already been described, in the various palaces which belonged to him, sometimes in one and sometimes in another.

The palace of Woodstock.

Among these palaces, one of the most beautiful was that of Woodstock. The engraving on the opposite page represents the buildings of the palace as they appeared some hundreds of years later than the time when Rosamond lived.

[Pg 55-6]

VIEW OF WOODSTOCK.
Rosamond's concealed cottage.
The construction of a labyrinth.
Deceptive paths.

In the days of Henry and Rosamond the palace of Woodstock was surrounded with very extensive and beautiful gardens and grounds. Somewhere upon these grounds the story was that Henry kept Rosamond in a concealed cottage. The entrance to the cottage was hidden in the depths of an almost impenetrable thicket, and could only be approached through a tortuous and intricate path, which led this way and that by an infinite number of turns, forming a sort of maze, made purposely to bewilder those attempting to pass in and out. Such a place was often made in those days in palace-grounds as a sort of ornament, or, rather, as an [Pg 57] amusing contrivance to interest the guests coming to visit the proprietor. It was called a labyrinth. A great many plans of labyrinths are found delineated in ancient books. The paths were not only so arranged as to twist and turn in every imaginable direction, but at every turn there were several branches made so precisely alike that there was nothing to distinguish one from the other. Of course, one of these roads was the right one, and led to the centre of the labyrinth, where there was a house, or a pretty seat with a view, or a garden, or a shady bower, or some other object of attraction, to reward those who should succeed in getting in. The other paths led nowhere, or, rather, they led on through various devious windings in all respects similar to those of the true path, until at length they came to a sudden stop, and the explorer was obliged to return.

The paths were separated from each other by dense hedges of thorn, or by high walls, so that it was impossible to pass from one to another except by walking regularly along.

It was in a house, entered through such a labyrinth as this, that Rosamond is said to have lived, on the grounds of the palace of Woodstock, while Queen Eleanora, as the avowed [Pg 58] wife and queen of King Henry, occupied the palace itself. Of course, the fact that such a lady was hidden on the grounds was kept a profound secret from the queen. If this story is true, there were probably other labyrinths on the grounds, and this one was so surrounded with trees and hedges, which connected it by insensible gradations with the groves and thickets of the park, that there was nothing to attract attention to it particularly, and thus a lady might have remained concealed in it for some time without awakening suspicion.

How Rosamond's concealment was discovered by the queen.
The subterranean passage.

At any rate, Rosamond did remain, it is supposed for a year or two, concealed thus, until at length the queen discovered the secret. The story is that the king found his way in and out the labyrinth by means of a clew of floss silk, and that the queen one day, when riding with the king in the park, observed this clew, a part of which had, in some way or other, become attached to his spur. She said nothing, but, watching a private opportunity, she followed the clew. It led by a very intricate path into the heart of the labyrinth. There the queen found a curiously-contrived door. The door was almost wholly concealed from view, but the queen discovered it and opened it. She found that it [Pg 59] led into a subterranean passage. The interest and curiosity of the queen were now excited more than ever, and she determined that the mystery should be solved. So she followed the passage, and was finally led by it to a place beyond the wall of the grounds, where there was a house in a very secluded spot surrounded by thickets. Here the queen found Rosamond sitting in a bower, and engaged in embroidering.

Uncertainties of the story.

She was now in a great rage both against Rosamond and against her husband. It was generally said that she poisoned Rosamond. The story was, that she took a cup of poison with her, and a dagger, and, presenting them both to Rosamond, compelled her to choose between them, and that Rosamond chose the poison, and, drinking it, died. This story, however, was not true, for it is now known that Rosamond lived many years after this time, though she was separated from the king. It is thought that her connection with the king continued for about two years after his marriage with Eleanora. She then left him. It may be that she did not know before that time that the king was married. She may have supposed that she was herself his lawful wife, as, indeed, it is possible that she may actually have been [Pg 60] so. At any rate, soon after she and Eleanora became acquainted with each other's existence, Rosamond retired to a convent, and lived there in complete seclusion all the rest of her days.

Rosamond retires to the convent of Godestow.

The name of this convent was Godestow. It was situated near Oxford. Rosamond became a great favorite with the nuns while she remained at the convent, which was nearly twenty years. During this time the king made many donations to the convent for Rosamond's sake, and the jealousy of the queen against her beautiful rival, of course, continued unabated. It was, indeed, this difficulty in respect to Rosamond that was one of the chief causes of the domestic trouble which always existed between Henry and the queen. The world at large have always been most disposed to sympathize with Rosamond in this quarrel. She was nearly of the king's own age, and his attachment to her arose, doubtless, from sincere affection; whereas the queen was greatly his senior, and had inveigled him, as it were, into a marriage with her, through motives of the most calculating and mercenary character.

Then, moreover, Rosamond either was, or was supposed to be, a lady of great gentleness and loveliness of spirit. She was very kind to [Pg 61] the poor, and while in the convent she was very assiduously devoted to her religious duties. Eleanora, on the other hand, was a very unprincipled and heartless woman, and she had been so loose and free in her own manner of living too, as every body said and believed, that it was with a very ill grace that she could find any fault with her husband.

The world's sympathy with Rosamond rather than with Eleanora.

Thus, under the circumstances of the case, the world has always been most inclined to sympathize with Rosamond rather than with the queen. The question which we ought to sympathize with depends upon which was really the wife of Henry. He may have been truly married to Rosamond, or at least some ceremony may have been performed which she honestly considered as a marriage. If so, she was innocent, and Henry was guilty for having virtually repudiated this marriage in order to connect himself with Eleanora for the sake of her kingdom. On the other hand, if she were not married to Henry, but used her arts to entice him away from his true wife, then she was deeply in fault. It is very difficult now to ascertain which of these suppositions is the correct one. In either case, Henry himself was guilty, toward the one or the other, of treacherously violating [Pg 62] his marriage vows—the most solemn vows, in some respects, that a man can ever assume.

The question of the validity of the marriage.

Rosamond had two children, named William and Geoffrey, and at one time in the course of his life Henry seemed to acknowledge that they were his only two children, thus admitting the validity of his marriage with Rosamond. This admission was contained in an expression which he used in addressing William on a field of battle when he came toward him at the head of his troop. "William," said he, "you are my true and legitimate son. The rest are nobodies." He may, it is true, have only intended to speak figuratively in saying this, meaning that William was the only one worthy to be considered as his son, or it may be that it was an inadvertent and hasty acknowledgment that Rosamond, and not Eleanora, was his true wife. As time rolled on, however, and the political arrangements arising out of the marriage with Eleanora and appointment of her sons to high positions in the state became more and more extended, the difficulties which the invalidation of the marriage with Eleanora would produce became very great, and immense interests were involved in sustaining it. Rosamond's rights, therefore, if she had any, were wholly overborne, [Pg 63] and she was allowed to linger and die in her nunnery as a private person.

Burial of Rosamond.
The bishop orders the remains to be removed.

When at length she died, the nuns, who had become greatly attached to her, caused her to be interred in an honorable manner in the chapel, but afterward the bishop of the diocese ordered the remains to be removed. He considered Rosamond as having never been married to the king, and he said that she was not a proper person to be the subject of monumental honors in the chapel of a society of nuns; so he sent the remains away, and ordered them to be interred in the common burying-ground. If Rosamond was what he supposed her to be, and if he removed the remains in a proper and respectful manner, he was right in doing what he did. His motive may have been, however, merely a desire to please the authorities of his time, who represented, of course, the heirs of Eleanora, by sealing the stamp of condemnation on the character and position of her rival.

[Pg 64]

FINAL BURIAL OF ROSAMOND.

The nuns bring back the remains to the chapel again.

But, though the authorities may have been pleased with the bishop's procedure, the nuns were not at all satisfied with it. They not only felt a strong personal affection for Rosamond, but, as a sisterhood, they felt grateful to her memory on account of the many benefactions which the convent had received from Henry on account of her residence there. So they seized the first opportunity to take up the remains again, which consisted now of dry bones alone, and, after perfuming them and inclosing them again in a new coffin, they deposited them once more under the pavement of the chapel, and [Pg 65] laid a slab, with a suitable inscription, over the spot to mark the place of the grave.

Rosamond's chamber.
Restoration of the house.

The house where Rosamond was concealed at Woodstock was regarded afterward with great interest, and there was a chamber in it that was for a long time known as Rosamond's Chamber. There remains a letter of one of the kings of England, written about a hundred years after this time, in which the king gives directions to have this house repaired, and particularly to have the chamber restored to a perfect condition. His orders are, that "the house beyond the gate in the new wall be built again, and that same chamber, called Rosamond's Chamber, be restored as before, and crystal plates"—that is, glass for the windows—"and marble, and lead be provided for it."

From that day to this the story of Rosamond has been regarded as one of the most interesting incidents of English history.

[Pg 66]

Chapter IV.

Accession of Richard to the Throne.

1189

The reverses of King Henry.

Richard was called to the throne when he was about thirty-two years of age by the sudden and unexpected death of his father. The death of his father took place under the most mournful circumstances imaginable. In the war which Richard and Philip, king of France, had waged against him, he had been unsuccessful. He had been defeated in the battles and outgeneraled in the manœuvres, and his barons, one after another, had abandoned him and taken part with the rebels. King Henry was an extremely passionate man, and the success of his enemies against him filled him with rage. This rage was rendered all the more violent by the thought that it was through the unnatural ingratitude of his own son, Richard, that all these calamities came upon him. In the anguish of his despair, he cursed the day of his birth, and uttered dreadful maledictions against his children.

[Pg 67]

Negotiating a peace.

At length he was reduced to such an extremity that he was obliged to submit to negotiations for peace, on just such terms as his enemies thought fit to impose. They made very hard conditions. The first attempt at negotiating the peace was made in an open field, where Philip and Henry met for the purpose, on horseback, attended by their retainers. Richard had the grace to keep away from this meeting, so as not to be an actual witness of the humiliation of his father, and so Philip and Henry were to conduct the conference by themselves.

The thunder-storm.

Henry's horsemanship.

The hard conditions of peace imposed by Philip and Richard.

The meeting was interrupted by a thunder-storm. At first the two kings did not intend to pay any heed to the storm, but to go on with their discussions without regarding it. Henry was a very great horseman, and spent almost his whole life in riding. One of his historians says that he never sat down except upon a saddle, unless it was when he was taking his meals. At any rate, he was almost always on horseback. He hunted on horseback, he fought on horseback, he traveled on horseback, and now he was holding a conference with his enemies on horseback, in the midst of a storm of lightning and rain. But his health had now become impaired, and his nerves, though they had always [Pg 68] seemed to be of iron, were beginning to give way under the dreadful shocks to which they had been exposed, so that he was now far less able to endure such exposures than he had been. At length a clap of thunder broke rattling immediately over his head, and the bolt seemed to descend directly between him and Philip as they sat upon their horses in the field. Henry reeled in the saddle, and would have fallen if his attendants had not seized and held him. They found that he was too weak and ill to remain any longer on the spot, and so they bore him away to his quarters, and then Philip and Richard sent him in writing the conditions which they were going to exact from him. The conditions were very humiliating indeed. They stripped him of a great portion of his possessions, and required him to hold others in subordination to Philip and to Richard. Finally, the last of the conditions was, that he was to give Richard the kiss of peace, and to banish from his heart all sentiments of animosity and anger against him.

The sick king.

Among other articles of the treaty was one binding him to pardon all the barons and other chief men who had gone over to Richard's side in the rebellion. As they read the articles [Pg 69] over to the king, while he was lying sick upon his bed, he asked, when they came to this one, to see the list of the names, that he might know who they were that had thus forsaken him. The name at the head of the list was that of his son John—his darling son John, to defend whose rights against the aggressions of Richard had been one of his chief motives in carrying on the war. The wretched father, on seeing this name, started up from his bed and gazed wildly around.

His distress at the conduct of John.

"Is it possible," he cried out, "that John, the child of my heart—he whom I have cherished more than all the rest, and for love of whom I have drawn down on mine own head all these troubles, has verily betrayed me?" They told him that it was even so.

"Then," said he, falling back helplessly on his bed, "then let every thing go as it will; I care no longer for myself or for any thing else in this world."

The palace at Chinon.
The imprecations of the dying king.

All this took place in Normandy, for it was Normandy that had been the chief scene of the war between the king and his son. At some little distance from the place where the king was now lying sick there was a beautiful rural palace, at a place called Chinon, which was situated [Pg 70] very pleasantly on the banks of a small branch of the Loire. This palace was one of the principal summer resorts of the dukes of Normandy, and the king caused himself now to be carried there, in order to seek repose. But instead of being cheered by the beautiful scenes that were around him at Chinon, or reinvigorated by the comforts and the attentions which he could there enjoy, he gradually sank into hopeless melancholy, and in a few days he began to feel that he was about to die. As he grew worse his mind became more and more excited, and his attendants from time to time heard him moaning, in his anguish, "Oh, shame! shame! I am a conquered king—a conquered king! Cursed be the day on which I was born, and cursed be the children that I leave behind me!"

The priests at his bedside endeavored to remonstrate with him against these imprecations. They told him that it was a dreadful thing for a father to curse his own children, and they urged him to retract what he had said. But he declared that he would not. He persisted in cursing all his children except Geoffrey Clifford, the son of Rosamond, who was then at his bedside, and who had never forsaken him. The king grew continually more and more excited [Pg 71] and disordered in mind, until at length he sank into a raving delirium, and in that state he died.

The heartless conduct of the courtiers of the dead king.

A dead king is a very helpless and insignificant object, whatever may have been the terror which he inspired while he was alive. As long as Henry continued to breathe, the attendants around him paid him great deference, and observed every possible form of obsequious respect, for they did not know but that he might recover, to live and reign, and lord it over them and their fortunes for fifteen or twenty years to come; but as soon as the breath was out of his body, all was over. Richard, his son, was now king, and from Henry nothing whatever was any longer to be hoped or feared. So the mercenary and heartless courtiers—the ministers, priests, bishops and barons—began at once to strip the body of all the valuables which the king had worn, and also to seize and appropriate every thing in the apartments of the palace which they could take away. These things were their perquisites, they said; it being customary, as they alleged, that the personal effects of a deceased king should be divided among those who were his attendants when he died. Having secured this plunder, these people disappeared, and it was with the utmost difficulty [Pg 72] that assistance enough could be procured to wrap the body in a winding-sheet, and to bring a hearse and horses to bear it away to the abbey where it was to be interred. Examples like this—of which the history of every monarchy is full—throw a great deal of light upon what is called the principle of loyalty in the hearts of those who attend upon kings.

Richard following the funeral train to the Abbey Fontevraud.

While the procession was on the way to the abbey where the body was to be buried, it was met by Richard, who, having heard of his father's death, came to join in the funeral solemnities. Richard followed the train until they arrived at the abbey. It was the Abbey Fontevraud, the ancient burial-place of the Norman princes. Arrived at the abbey, the body was laid out upon the bier, and the face was uncovered, in order that Richard might once more look upon his father's features; but the countenance was so distorted with the scowling expression of rage and resentment which it had worn during the sufferer's last hours, that Richard turned away in horror from the dreadful spectacle.

Richard immediately secures the succession to the throne.

But Richard soon drove away from his mind the painful thoughts which the sight of his father's face must have awakened, and turned his [Pg 73] attention at once to the business which now pressed upon him. He, of course, was heir both to the crown of England and also to all his father's possessions in Normandy, and he felt that he must act promptly, in order to secure his rights. It is true that there was nobody to dispute his claim, unless it was his brother John, for the two sons of Rosamond, Geoffrey and William Clifford, did not pretend to any rights of inheritance. Richard had some fears of John, and he thought it necessary to take decisive measures to guard against any plots that John might be disposed to form. He sent at once to England, and ordered that his mother should be released from her imprisonment, and invested her with power to act as regent there until he should come. In the mean time, he himself remained in Normandy, and devoted himself to arranging and regulating the affairs of his French possessions. This was the wisest course for him to pursue, for there was no one in England to dispute his claims to that kingdom. On the Continent the case was different. His neighbor, Philip, King of France, was ready to take advantage of any opportunity to get possession of such provinces on the Continent as might be within his reach.

[Pg 74]

Sorrow often results in happiness.

It was certainly a good deed in Richard to liberate his mother from her captivity, and to exalt her as he did to a position of responsibility and honor. Eleanora fulfilled the trust which he reposed in her in a very faithful and successful manner. The long period of confinement and suffering which she had endured seems to have exerted a very favorable influence upon her mind. Indeed, it is very often the case that sorrow and trouble have this effect. A life of prosperity and pleasure makes us heartless, selfish, and unfeeling, while sorrow softens the heart, and disposes us to compassionate the woes of others, and to do what we can to relieve them.

45

Eleanora queen regent.
Her change of character.

Eleanora was queen regent in England for two months, and during that time she employed her power in a very beneficent manner. She released many unhappy prisoners, and pardoned many persons who had been convicted of political crimes. The truth is that probably, as she found herself drawing toward the close of life, and looked back upon her past career, and remembered her many crimes, her unfaithfulness to both her husbands, and especially her unnatural conduct in instigating her sons to rebel against their father, her heart was filled [Pg 75] with remorse, and she found some relief from her anguish in these tardy efforts to relieve suffering which might, in some small degree, repair the evils that she had brought upon the land by the insurrections and wars of which she had been the cause. She bitterly repented of the hostility that she had shown toward her husband, and of the countless wrongs that she had inflicted upon him. While he was alive, and she was engaged in her contests with him, the excitement that she was under blinded her mind; but now that he was dead, her passion subsided, and she mourned for him with bitter grief. She distributed alms in a very abundant manner to the poor to induce them to pray for the repose of his soul. While doing these things she did not neglect the affairs of state. She made all the necessary arrangements for the immediate administration of the government, and she sent word to all the barons, and also to the bishops, and other great public functionaries, informing them that Richard was coming to assume the government of the realm, and summoning them to assemble and make ready to receive him. In about two months Richard came.

Richard's return to England.
Richard's proposed crusade.

Before Richard arrived in England, however, [Pg 76] he had formed the plan, in connection with Philip, the King of France, of going on a crusade. Richard was a wild and desperate man, and he loved fighting for its own sake; and inasmuch as now, since his father was dead, and his claim to the crown of England, and to all his possessions in Normandy, was undisputed, there seemed to be nobody for him to fight at home, he conceived the design of organizing a grand expedition to go to the Holy Land and fight the Saracens.

John was very much pleased with this idea. "If Richard goes to Palestine," said he to himself, "ten to one he will get killed, and then I shall be King of England."

John's dissimulation.

So John was ready to do every thing in his power to favor the plan of the crusade. He pretended to be very submissive and obedient to his brother, and to acknowledge his sovereign power as king. He aided the king as much as he could in making his arrangements and in concocting all his plans.

A delusion.

The first thing was to provide funds. A great deal of money was required for these expeditions. Ships were to be bought and equipped for the purpose of transporting the troops to the East. Arms and ammunition [Pg 77] were to be provided, and large supplies of food. Then the princes, and barons, and knights who were to accompany the expedition required very expensive armor, and costly trappings and equipments of all sorts; for, though the pretense was that they were going out to fight for the recovery of the Holy Sepulchre under the influence of religious zeal, the real motive which animated them was love of glory and display. Thus it happened that the expense which a sovereign incurred in fitting out a crusade was enormous.

The treasures of the crown.

Accordingly, King Richard, immediately on his arrival in England, proceeded at once to Winchester, where his father, King Henry, had kept his treasures. Richard found a large sum of money there in gold and silver coin, and besides this there were stores of plate, of jewelry, and of precious gems of great value. Richard caused all the money to be counted in his presence, and an exact inventory to be made of all the treasures. He then placed the whole under the charge of trusty officers of his own, whom he appointed to take care of them.

Circumstances alter cases.
Accomplices ill rewarded.

The next thing that Richard did was to discard and dismiss all his own former friends and adherents — the men who had taken part with [Pg 78] him in his rebellions against his father. "Men that would join me in rebelling against my father," thought he to himself, "would join any body else, if they thought they could gain by it, in rebelling against me." So he concluded that they were not to be trusted. Indeed now, in the altered circumstances in which he was placed, he could see the guilt of rebellion and treason, though he had been blind to it before, and he actually persecuted and punished some of those who had been his confederates in his former crimes. A great many cases analogous to this have occurred in English history. Sons have often made themselves the centre and soul of all the opposition in the realm against their father's government, and have given their fathers a great deal of trouble by so doing; but then, in all such cases, the moment that the father dies the son immediately places himself at the head of the regularly-constituted authorities of the realm, and abandons all his old companions and friends, treating them sometimes with great severity. His eyes are opened to the wickedness of making opposition to the sovereign power now that the sovereign power is vested in himself, and he disgraces and punishes his own former friends for the crime of having aided him in his undutiful behavior.

[Pg 79]

Chapter V.

The Coronation.

1189

The massacre of the Jews.

I t was now time that the coronation should take place, and arrangements were accordingly made for performing this ceremony with great magnificence in Westminster Abbey. The day of the ceremony acquired a dreadful celebrity in history in consequence of a great massacre of the Jews, which resulted from an insurrection and riot that broke out in Westminster and London immediately after the crowning of the king. The Jews had been hated and abhorred by all the Christian nations of Europe for many ages. Since they were not believers in Christianity, they were considered as little better than infidels and heathen, and the government that oppressed and persecuted them the most was considered as doing the greatest service to the cause of religion.

Their social position.
The history of the commercial character of the Jews.

One very curious result followed from the legal disabilities that the Jews were under. They could not own land, and they were restricted [Pg 80] also very much in respect to nearly all the avocations open to other men. They consequently learned gradually to become dealers in money and in jewels, this being almost the only reputable calling that was left open to them. There was another great advantage, too, for them, in dealing in property of this kind, and that was, that comprising, as such property does, great value in small bulk, it could easily be concealed, and removed from place to place whenever it was specially endangered by the edicts of governments or the hostility of enemies.

From these and similar reasons the Jews became bankers and money-lenders, and they are to this day the richest bankers and the greatest money-lenders in the world. The most powerful emperors and kings often depend upon them for the supplies that they require to carry on their great undertakings or to defray the expenses of their wars.

The persecution of the Jews in France.

The Jews had gradually increased in numbers and influence in France until the time of the accession of Philip, and then he determined to extirpate them from the realm; so he issued an edict by which they were all banished from the kingdom, their property was confiscated, [Pg 81] and every person that owed them money was released from all obligation to pay them. Of course, a great many of their debtors would pay them, notwithstanding this release, from the influence of that natural sense of justice which, in all nations and in all ages, has a very great control in human hearts; still, there were others who would, of course, avail themselves of this opportunity to defraud their creditors of what was justly their due; and being obliged, too, at the same time, to fly precipitately from the country in consequence of the decree of banishment, the poor Jews were reduced to a state of extreme distress.

Conciliating the king.

Now the Jews of England, when Henry died and Richard succeeded him, began to be afraid that the new king would follow Philip's example, and in order to prevent this, and to conciliate Richard's favor, they determined to send a delegation to him at Westminster, at the time of his coronation, with rich presents which had been procured by contributions made by the wealthy. Accordingly, on the day of the coronation, when the great crowds of people assembled at Westminster to honor the occasion, these Jews came among them.

A description of the ceremony of coronation.

The ceremony of the coronation was performed [Pg 82] in the following manner: The king, in entering the church and proceeding up toward the high altar, walked upon a rich cloth laid down for him, which had been dyed with the famous Tyrian purple. Over his head was a beautifully-wrought canopy of silk, supported by four long lances. These lances were borne by four great barons of the realm. A great nobleman, the Earl of Albemarle, bore the crown, and walked with it before the king as he advanced toward the altar. When the earl reached the altar he placed the crown upon it. The Archbishop of Canterbury stood before the altar to receive the king as he approached, and then administered the usual oath to him.

The oath was in three parts:

1. That all the days of his life he would bear peace, honor, and reverence to God and the Holy Church, and to all the ordinances thereof.

2. That he would exercise right, justice, and law on the people unto him committed.

3. That he would abrogate wicked laws and perverse customs, if any such should be brought into his kingdom, and that he would enact good laws, and the same in good faith keep, without mental reservation.

The ampulla.

Having taken this oath, the king removed [Pg 83] his upper garment, and put golden sandals upon his feet, and then was anointed by the archbishop with the holy oil on his head, breast, and shoulders. This oil was poured from a rich vessel called an *ampulla*. [C]

The coronation.

The anointing having been performed, the king received various articles of royal dress and decoration from the hands of the great nobles around him, who officiated as servitors on the occasion, and with their assistance put them on. When thus robed and adorned, he advanced up the steps of the altar. As he went up, the archbishop adjured him in the name of the living God not to assume the crown unless he was fully resolved to keep the oaths that he had sworn. Richard again solemnly called God to witness that he would faithfully keep them, and then advancing to the altar, he took the crown and put it into the hands of the archbishop, who then placed it upon his head, and thus the coronation ceremony was completed.

Presents.
Hostility and jealousy of the people.

The people who had presents for the king now approached and offered them to him. [Pg 84] Among them came the Jews. Their presents were very rich and valuable, and the king received them very gladly, although in announcing the arrangements for the ceremony he had declared that no Jew and no woman was to be allowed to be present. Notwithstanding this prohibition, the Jewish deputation had come in and offered their presents among the rest. There was, however, a great murmuring among the crowd in respect to them, and a great desire to drive them out. This crowd consisted chiefly, of course, of barons, earls, knights, and other great dignitaries of the realm, for very few of the lower ranks would be admitted to see the ceremony; and these people, in addition to the usual religious prejudice against the Jews, had many of them been exasperated against the bankers and money-lenders on account of difficulties that they had had with them in relation to money that they had borrowed, and to the high interest which they had been compelled to pay. Some wise observer of the working of human passions has said that men always hate more or less those to whom they owe money. This is a reason why there should ordinarily be very few pecuniary transactions between friends.

An altercation.

At length, as one of the Jews who was outside [Pg 85] was attempting to go in, a by-stander at the gate cried out, "Here comes a Jew!" and struck at him. This excited the passions of the rest, and they struck and pushed the poor Jew in order to drive him back; and at the same time a general outcry against the Jews arose, and spread into the interior of the hall. The people there, glad of the opportunity afforded them by the excitement, began to assault the Jews and drive them out; and as they came out at the door beaten and bruised, a rumor was raised that they had been expelled by the king's orders. This rumor, as it spread through the streets, was soon changed into a report that the king had ordered all the unbelievers to be destroyed; and so, whenever a Jew was found in the street, a riot was raised about him, he was assaulted with sticks and stones, cruelly beaten, and if he was not killed, he was driven to seek refuge in his home, wounded and bleeding.

Hunting out the Jews.

In the mean time, the news that the king had ordered all the Jews to be killed spread rapidly over the town, and in the evening crowds collected, and after murdering all the Jews that they could find in the streets, they gathered round their houses, and finally broke into them [Pg 86] and killed the inhabitants. In some cases where the houses were strong, the Jews barricaded the doors and the mob could not get in. In such cases they brought combustibles, and piled them up before the windows and doors, and then, setting them on fire, they burned the houses to the ground, and men, women, and children were consumed together in the flames. If any of the unhappy wretches burning in these fires attempted to escape by leaping from the windows, the mob below held up spears and lances for them to fall upon.

The terrors of the massacre.

There were so many of these fires in the course of the night that the whole sky was illuminated, and at one time there was danger that the flames would spread so as to produce a general conflagration. Indeed, as the night passed on, the excitement became more and more violent, until at length the streets, in all the quarters where Jews resided, were filled with the shouts of the mob, raving in demoniacal phrensy, and with the screams of the terrified and dying sufferers, and the crackling of the lurid flames in which they were burning.

Indifference of the king.
The mob unchecked.

The king, in the mean time, was carousing with his lords and barons in the great banqueting-hall at Westminster, and for a time took [Pg 87] no notice of these disturbances. He seemed to consider them as of very little moment. At length, however, in the course of the night, he sent an officer and a few men to suppress the riot. But it was too late. The mob paid no heed to remonstrances which came from the leader of so small a force, but, on the other hand, threatened to kill the soldiers too, if they did not go away. So the officer returned to the king, and the riot went on undisturbed until about two o'clock of the next day, when it gradually ceased from the mere weariness and exhaustion of the people.

The impunity of the rioters.

A few of the men who had been engaged in this riot were afterward brought to trial, and three were hung, not for murdering Jews, but for burning some Christian houses, which, either by mistake or accident, took fire in the confusion and were burned with the rest. This was all that was ever done to punish this dreadful crime.

King Richard's edict.

In justice to King Richard, however, it must be stated that he issued an edict after this forbidding that the Jews should be injured or maltreated any more. He took the whole people, he said, thenceforth under his special protection, and all men were strictly forbidden to harm [Pg 88] them personally, or to molest them in the possession of their property.

And this was the terrible coronation scene which signalized the investiture of Richard with the crown and the royal robes of England.

[Pg 89]

Chapter VI.

Preparations for the Crusade.

1189

Richard was thirty-two years of age at his accession.

A t the time of his accession to the throne, Richard, as has already been remarked, was about thirty-two years of age. On the following page you have a portrait of him, with the crown upon his head.

This portrait is taken from a sculpture on his tomb, and is undoubtedly a good representation of him as he appeared when he was alive.

[Pg 90]

PORTRAIT
OF RICHARD I.
His ardent desires for distinction in crusades.
Motives of the crusaders.
A strange delusion.

The first thing that Richard turned his attention to, when he found himself securely seated on his throne, was the preparation for a crusade. It had been the height of his ambition for a long time to lead a crusade. It was undoubtedly through the influence of his mother, and of her early conversations with him, that he imbibed his extraordinary eagerness to seek adventures in the Holy Land. She had been a crusader herself during her first marriage, as has already been related in this volume, and she had undoubtedly, in Richard's early life, entertained him with a thousand stories of what she had seen, and of the romantic adventures which she had met with there. These stories, and the various conversations which arose out of them, kindled Richard's youthful imagination with ardent desires to go and distinguish himself on the same field. These desires had been [Pg 91] greatly increased as Richard grew up to manhood by observing the exalted military glory to which successful crusaders attained. And then, besides this, Richard was endued with a sort of reckless and lion-like courage, which led him to look upon danger as a sport, and made him long for a field where there were plenty of enemies to fight, and enemies so abhorred by the whole Christian world that he could indulge in the excitement of hatred and rage against them without any restraint whatever. He could there satiate himself, too, with the luxury of killing men without any misgiving of conscience, or, at least, without any condemnation on the part of his fellow-men, for it was understood throughout Christendom that the crimes committed against the Saracens in the Holy Land were committed in the name of Christ. What a strange delusion! To think of honoring the memory of the meek and lowly Jesus by utterly disregarding his peaceful precepts and his loving and gentle example, and going forth in thousands to the work of murder, rapine, and devastation, in order to get possession of his tomb.

The preparations.
Navies.
Armies.
Accoutrements.
Customs of old times.

In preparing for the crusade, the first and [Pg 92] most important thing to be attended to, in Richard's view, was the raising of money. A great deal of money would be required, as has already been intimated, to fit out the expedition on the magnificent scale which Richard intended. There was a fleet of ships to be built and equipped, and stores of provisions to be put on board. There were armies to be levied and paid, and immense expenses were to be incurred in the manufacture of arms and ammunition. The armor and the arms used in those days, especially those worn by knights and noblemen, and the caparisons of the horses, were extremely costly. The armor was fashioned with great labor and skill out of plates or rings of steel, and the helmets, and the bucklers, and the swords, and all the military trappings of the horses and horsemen, being fashioned altogether by hand, required great labor and skill in the artisan who made them; and then, moreover, it was customary to decorate them very profusely with embroidery, and gold, and gems. At the present day, men display their wealth in the costliness of their houses, and the gorgeousness and luxury of the furniture which they contain. It is not considered in good taste—except for ladies—to make a display of wealth [Pg 93] upon the person. In those days, however, the reverse was the case. The knights and barons lived in the rudest stone castles, dark and frowning without, and meagerly furnished and comfortless within, while all the means of display which the owners possessed were lavished in arming and decorating themselves and their horses magnificently for the field of battle.

Richard's reckless course.

For all these things Richard knew that he should require a large sum of money, and he proceeded at once to carry into effect the most wasteful and reckless measures for obtaining it. His father, Henry the Second, had in various ways acquired a great many estates in different parts of the kingdom, which estates he had added to the royal domains. These Richard at once proceeded to sell to whomsoever would give the most for them. In this manner he disposed of a great number of castles, fortresses, and towns, so as greatly to diminish the value of the crown property. The purchasers of this property, if they had not money enough of their own to pay for what they bought, would borrow of the Jews. Some of the king's counselors remonstrated with him against this wasteful policy, but he replied that he needed money so much for the crusade, that, if necessary, he [Pg 94] would sell the city of London itself to raise it, if he could only find a man rich enough to be the purchaser.

Richard sold lands, offices, and titles of honor.

After having raised as much money as he could by the sale of the royal lands, the next resource to which Richard turned was the sale of public offices and titles of honor. He looked about the country for wealthy men, and he offered them severally high office on condition of their paying large sums of money into the treasury as a consideration for them. He sold titles of nobility, too, in the same way. If any man who was not rich held a high or important office, he would find some pretext for removing him, and then would offer the office for sale. One of the historians of those times says that at this period Richard's presence-chamber became a regular place of trade—like the counting-room of a merchant or an exchange—where every thing that could be derived from the bounty of the crown or bestowed by the royal prerogative was offered for sale in open market to the man who would give the best bargain for it.

Extortion under pretense of public justice.

Another of the modes which the king adopted for raising money, and in some respects the worst of all, was to impose fines as a punishment [Pg 95] for crime, and then, in order to make the fines produce as much as possible, every imaginable pretext was resorted to to charge wealthy persons with offenses, with a view of exacting large sums from them as the penalty. It was said that a great officer of state was charged with some offense, and was put in prison and not released until he had paid a fine of three thousand pounds.

One of the worst of these cases was that of his half-brother Geoffrey, the son of Rosamond. Geoffrey had been appointed Archbishop of York in accordance with the wish that his father Henry had expressed on his death-bed. Richard pretended to be displeased with this. Perhaps he wished to have had that office to dispose of like the rest. At any rate, he exacted a very large sum from Geoffrey as the condition on which he would "grant him his peace," as he termed it, and Geoffrey paid the money.

Creating a regency.
Richard's regents.
John's acquiescence.

When, by these and other similar means, Richard had raised all that he could in England, he prepared to cross the Channel into Normandy, in order to see what more he could do there. Before he went, however, he had first to make arrangements for a regency to govern England [Pg 96] while he should be away. This is always the custom in monarchical countries. Whenever, for any reason, the true sovereign can not personally exercise the supreme power, whether from minority, insanity, long-continued sickness, or protracted absence from the realm, a regency, as it is called, is created to govern the kingdom in his stead. The person appointed to act as regent is usually some near relation of the king. Richard's brother John hoped to be made regent, but this did not suit Richard's views, for he wished to make this office the means, as all the others had been, of raising money, and John had no money to give. For the same reason, he could not appoint his mother, who in other respects would have been a very suitable person. So Richard contrived a sort of middle course. He sold the nominal regency to two wealthy courtiers, whom he associated together for the purpose. One was a bishop, and the other was an earl. It may, perhaps, be too much to say that he directly sold them the office, but, at any rate, he appointed them jointly to it, and under the arrangement that was made he received a large sum of money. He, however, stipulated that John, and also his mother, should have a large [Pg 97] share of influence in deciding upon all the measures of the government. John would have been by no means satisfied with this divided and uncertain share of power were it not that he was so desirous of favoring the expedition in every possible way, in hopes that if Richard could once get to the Holy Land he would soon perish there, and that then he should be king altogether. It was of comparatively little consequence who was regent in the mean time. So he resolved to make no objection to any plan that the king might propose.

The time for sailing appointed.

Richard was now ready to cross to Normandy; but just before he went there came a deputation from Philip to consult with him in respect to the plans of the crusade, and to fix upon the time for setting out. The time proposed by Philip was the latter part of March. It was now late in the fall. It would not be safe to set out before March on account of the inclemency of the season, and Richard supposed that he should have ample time to complete his preparations by the time that Philip named. So both parties agreed to it, and they took a solemn oath on both sides that they would all be ready without fail.

Richard crosses the Channel.

Soon after this Richard took leave of his [Pg 98] friends, and, accompanied by a long retinue of earls, barons, knights, and other adventurers who were to accompany him to the Holy Land, he left England, and crossed the Channel to Normandy.

Fears of treachery.
The treaty of alliance between Richard and Philip.

In such cases as this there are always a great many last words to be said and a great many last arrangements to be made, and Richard found it necessary to see his mother and his brother John again before finally taking his departure from Europe. So he sent for them to come to Normandy, and there another great council of state was held, at which every thing in relation to the internal affairs of his dominions was finally arranged. There was still one other danger to be guarded against, and that was some treachery on the part of Philip himself. So little reliance did these valiant champions of Christianity place in each other in those days, that both Richard and Philip, in joining together to form this expedition, had many misgivings and suspicions in respect to each other's honesty. Undoubtedly neither of them would have thought it safe to leave his dominions and go on a crusade unless the other had been going too. The one left behind would have been sure to have found some pretext, during the absence [Pg 99] of his neighbor, to invade his dominions and plunder him of some of his possessions. This was one reason why the two kings had agreed to go together; and now, as an additional safeguard, they made a formal treaty of alliance and fraternity, in which they bound themselves by the most solemn oaths to stand by each other, and to be faithful and true to each other to the last. They agreed that each would defend the life and honor of the other on all occasions; that neither would desert the other in the hour of danger; and that, in respect to the dominions that they were respectively to leave behind them, neither would form any designs against the other, but that Philip would cherish and protect the rights of Richard even as he would protect his own city of Paris, and that Richard would do the like by Philip, even as he would protect his own city of Rouen.

It is a curious circumstance that in this treaty Richard should name Rouen, and not London, as his principal capital. It confirms what is known in many other ways, that the kings of this line, reigning over both Normandy and England, considered Normandy as the chief centre of their power, and England as subordinate. It may be, however, that one reason [Pg 100] why Rouen was named in this instance may have been because it was nearer to the dominions of the King of France, and so better known to him.

Completion of the preparations.

This treaty was signed in February, and the preparations were now nearly complete for setting forth on the expedition in March, at the appointed time.

[Pg 101]

Chapter VII.

The Embarkation.

1190

The plan of embarking the troops.

The plan which Richard had formed for conveying his expedition to the Holy Land was to embark it on board a fleet of ships which he was sending round to Marseilles for this purpose, with orders to await him there. Marseilles is in the south of France, not far from the Mediterranean Sea. Richard might have embarked his troops in the English Channel; but that, as the reader will see from looking on the map of Europe, would require them to take a long sea voyage around the coasts of France and Spain, and through the Straits of Gibraltar. Richard thought it best to avoid this long circuit for his troops, and so he sent the ships round, with no more men on board than necessary to manœuvre them, while he marched his army across France by land.

The English fleet.

As for Philip, he had no ships of his own. England was a maritime country, and had long possessed a fleet. This fleet had been very much increased by the exertions of Henry the [Pg 102] Second, Richard's father, who had built several new ships, some of them of very large size, expressly for the purpose of transporting troops to Palestine. Henry himself did not live to execute his plans, and so he left his ships for Richard.

The French forces.

France, on the other hand, was not then a maritime country. Most of the harbors on the northern coast belonged to Normandy, and even at the south the ports did not belong to the King of France. Philip, therefore, had no fleet of his own, but he had made arrangements with the republic of Genoa to furnish him with ships, and so his plan was to march over the mountains to that city and embark there, while Richard should go south to Marseilles.

Richard's rules.

Richard drew up a curious set of rules and regulations for the government of this fleet while it was making the passage. Some of the rules were the following:

1. That if any man killed another, the murderer was to be lashed to the dead body and buried alive with it, if the murder was committed in port or on the land. If the crime was committed at sea, then the two bodies, bound together as before, were to be launched overboard.

[Pg 103] 2. If any man, with a knife or with any other weapon, struck another so as to draw blood, then he was to be punished by being ducked three times over head and ears by being let down from the yard-arm of the ship into the sea.

3. For all sorts of profane and abusive language, the punishment was a fine of an ounce of silver for each offense.

4. Any man convicted of theft, or "pickerie" as it was called, was to have his head shaved and hot pitch poured over it, and upon that the feathers of some pillow or cushion were to be shaken. The offender was then to be turned ashore on the first land that the ship might reach, and there be abandoned to his fate.

The origin of tarring and feathering.

The penalty named in this last article is the first instance in which any account of the punishment of tarring and feathering is mentioned, and this is supposed to be the origin of that extraordinary and very cruel mode of punishment.

Command of the fleet.

The king put the fleet under the command of three grand officers of his court, and he commanded all his seamen and marines to obey them strictly in all things, as they would obey the king himself if he had been on board.

The fleet dispersed by a storm.
A delay in Lisbon.

The fleet met with a great variety of adventures on its way to Marseilles. It had not proceeded [Pg 104] far before a great tempest arose, and scattered the ships in every direction. At last, a considerable number of them succeeded in making their way, in a disabled condition, into the Tagus, in order to seek succor in Lisbon. The King of Portugal was at this time at war with the Moors, who had come over from Africa and invaded his dominions. He proposed to the Crusaders on board the ships to wait a little while, and assist him in fighting the Moors. "They are as great infidels," said he, "as any that you will find in the Holy Land." The commanders of the fleet acceded to this proposal, but the crews, when they were landed, soon made so many riots in Lisbon, and involved themselves in such frequent and bloody affrays with the people of the city, that the King of Portugal was soon eager to send them away; so, in due time, they embarked again, in order to continue their voyage.

The rendezvous at Vezelai.
Devastation by the armies.

In the mean time, while the fleet was thus going round by sea, Richard and Philip were engaged in assembling their forces and making preparation to march by land. The two armies, when finally organized, came together at a place of rendezvous called Vezelai, where there were great plains suitable for the camping-ground of [Pg 105] a great military force. Vezelai was on the road to Lyons, and the armies, after they had met, marched in company to the latter city. The number of troops assembled was very great. The united army amounted, it is said, to one hundred thousand men. This was a very large force for those days. The great difficulty was to find provision for them from day to day during the march. Supplies of provisions for such a host can not be carried far, so that armies are obliged to live on the produce of the country that they march through, which is collected for this purpose by foragers from day to day. The allied armies, as they moved slowly on, impoverished and distressed the whole country through which they passed, by devouring every thing that the people had in store. At length, after marching together for some time, they came to the place where the roads separated, and King Philip turned off to the left in order to proceed through the passes of the Alps toward Genoa, while Richard and his hosts proceeded southward toward Marseilles.

When he reached Marseilles, Richard found that his fleet had not arrived. The delay was occasioned by the storm, and the subsequent detention of the crews at Lisbon. And yet this [Pg 106] was very long after the time originally appointed for the sailing of the expedition. The time first appointed was the last of March; but Philip could not go at that time, on account of the death of his queen, which took place just before the appointed period. Nor was Richard himself ready. It was not until the thirtieth of August that the fleet arrived at Marseilles.

Richard goes to the East in advance of his fleet.

When Richard found that the fleet had not come he was greatly disappointed. He had no means of knowing when to expect it, for there were no postal or other communications across the country in those days, as now, by which tidings could be conveyed to him. He waited eight days very impatiently, and then concluded to go on himself toward the East, and leave orders for the fleet to follow him. So he hired ten large vessels and twenty galleys of the merchants of Marseilles, and in these he embarked a portion of his forces, leaving the rest to come in the great fleet when it should arrive. They were to proceed to Messina in Sicily, where Richard was to join them. With the vessels that he had hired he proceeded along the coast to Genoa, where he found Philip, the French king, who had arrived there safely before him by land.

[Pg 107]

The rendezvous at Messina.
Joanna.
Richard's visit.

From Marseilles to Genoa the course lies toward the northeast along the coast of France. Thence, in going toward Messina, it turns toward the southeast, and follows the coast of Italy. The route may be traced very easily on any map of modern Europe. The reason why Messina had been appointed as the great intermediate rendezvous of the fleet was two-fold. In the first place, it was a convenient port for this purpose, being a good harbor, and being favorably situated about midway of the voyage. Then, besides, Richard had a sister residing there. Her name was Joanna. She had married the king of the country. Her husband had died, it is true, and she was, at that time in some sense retired from public life. She was, indeed, in some distress, for the throne had been seized by a certain Tancred, who was her enemy, and, as she maintained, not the rightful successor of her husband. So Richard resolved, in stopping at Messina, to inquire into and redress his sister's wrongs; or, rather, he thought the occasion offered him a favorable opportunity to interfere in the affairs of Sicily, and to lord it over the government and people there in his usual arrogant and domineering manner.

[Pg 108]

King Richard's excursions.
Ostia.

After waiting a short time at Genoa, Richard set sail again in one of his small vessels, and proceeded to the southward along the coast of Italy. He touched at several places on the coast, in order to visit celebrated cities or other places of interest. He sailed up the River Arno, which you will find, on the map, flowing into the Gulf of Genoa a little to the northward of Leghorn. There are two renowned cities on this river, which are very much visited by tourists and travelers of the present day, Florence and Pisa. Pisa is near the mouth of the river. Florence is much farther inland. Richard sailed up as far as Pisa. After visiting that city, he returned again to the mouth of the river, and then proceeded on his way down the coast until he came to the Tiber, and entered that river. He landed at Ostia, a small port near the mouth of it—the port, in fact, of Rome. One reason why he landed at Ostia was that the galley in which he was making the voyage required some repairs, and this was a convenient place for making them.

A quarrel.
Why Richard quarreled with the bishop.

Perhaps, too, it was his intention to visit Rome; but while at Ostia he became involved in a quarrel with the bishop that resided there, which led him at length to leave Ostia abruptly, [Pg 109] and to refuse to go to Rome. The cause of the quarrel was the bishop's asking him to pay some money that he owed the Pope. In all the Catholic countries of Europe, in those days, there were certain taxes and fees that were collected for the Pope, the income from which was of great importance in making up the papal revenues. Now Richard, in his eagerness to secure all the money he could obtain in England to supply his wants for the crusade, had appropriated to his own use certain of these church funds, and the bishop now called upon him to reimburse them. This application, as might have been expected, made Richard extremely angry. He assailed the bishop with the most violent and abusive language, and charged all sorts of corruption and wickedness against the papal government itself. These charges may have been true, but the occasion of being called upon to pay a debt was not the proper time for making them. To make the faults or misconduct of others, whether real or pretended, an excuse for not rendering them their just dues, is a very base proceeding.

As soon as Richard's galley was repaired, he embarked on board of it in a rage, and sailed away. The next point at which he landed was Naples.

[Pg 110]

Naples and Vesuvius.
The crypt.

Richard was greatly delighted with the city of Naples, which, rising as it does from the shores of an enchanting bay, and near the base of the volcano Vesuvius, has long been celebrated for the romantic beauty of its situation. Richard remained at Naples several days. There is an account of his going, while there, to perform his devotions in the crypt of a church. The crypt is a subterranean apartment beneath the church, the floors above it, as well as the pillars and walls of the church, being supported by immense piers and arches, which give the crypt the appearance of a dungeon. The place is commonly used for tombs and places of sepulture for the dead. In the crypt where Richard worshiped at Naples, the dead bodies were arranged in niches all around the walls. They were dressed as they had been when alive, and their countenances, dry and shriveled, were exposed to view, presenting a ghastly and horrid spectacle. It was such means as these that were resorted to, in the Middle Ages, for making religious impressions on the minds of men.

Salerno.
Richard's visit there.

After spending some days in Naples, Richard concluded that he would continue his route; but, instead of embarking at once on board his galley, he determined to go across the mountains [Pg 111] by land to Salerno, which town lies on the sea-coast at some distance south of Naples. By looking at any map of Italy, you will observe that a great promontory puts out into the sea just below Naples, forming the Gulf of Salerno on the south side of it. The pass through the mountains which Richard followed led across the neck of this promontory. His galley, together with the other galleys that accompanied him, he sent round by water. There was a great deal to interest him at Salerno, for it was a place where many parties of crusaders, Normans among the rest, had landed before, and they had built churches and monasteries, and founded institutions of learning there, all of which Richard was much interested in visiting.

The fleet.
Richard pursuing his journey along the coast of the Mediterranean.

He accordingly remained in Salerno several days, until at length his fleet of galleys, which had come round from Naples by sea, arrived. Richard, however, in the mean time, had found traveling by land so agreeable, that he concluded to continue his journey in that way, leaving his fleet to sail down the coast, keeping all the time as near as possible to the shore. The king himself rode on upon the land, accompanied by a very small troop of attendants. His way led him sometimes among the mountains of the interior, [Pg 112] and sometimes near the margin of the shore. At some points, where the road approached so near to the cliffs as to afford a good view of the sea, the fleet of galleys were to be seen in the offing prosperously pursuing their voyage.

[Pg 113-4]

RICHARD PURSUING HIS JOURNEY.
Richard's tyrannical disposition.

The king went on in this way till he reached Calabria, which is the country situated in the southern portion of Italy. The roads here were very bad, and as the autumn was now coming on, many of the streams became so swollen with rains that it was difficult sometimes for him to proceed on his way. At one time, while he was thus journeying, he became involved in a difficulty with a party of peasants which was extremely discreditable to him, and exhibits his character in a very unfavorable light. It seems that he was traveling by an obscure country road, in company with only a single attendant, when he happened to pass by a village, where he was told a peasant lived who had a very fine hunting hawk or falcon. Hunting by means of these hawks was a common amusement of the knights and nobles of those days; and Richard, when he heard about this hawk, said that a plain countryman had no business with such a bird. He declared that he would go to his [Pg 115] house and take it away from him. This act, so characteristic of the despotic arrogance which marked Richard's character, shows that the reckless ferocity for which he was so renowned was not softened or alleviated by any true and genuine nobleness or generosity. For a rich and powerful king thus to rob a poor, helpless peasant, and on such a pretext too, was as base a deed as we can well conceive a royal personage to perform.

Stealing the falcon.
Richard flees to a priory to escape the peasants.

Richard at once proceeded to carry his design into execution. He went into the peasant's house, and having, under some pretext or other, got possession of the falcon, he began to ride away with the bird on his wrist. The peasant called out to him to give him back his bird. Richard paid no attention to him, but rode on. The peasant then called for help, and other villagers joining him, they followed the king, each one having seized in the mean time such weapons as came most readily to hand. They surrounded the king in order to take the falcon away, while he attempted to beat them off with his sword. Pretty soon he broke his sword by a blow which he struck at one of the peasants, and then he was in a great measure defenseless. His only safety now was in flight. He contrived [Pg 116] to force his way through the circle that surrounded him, and began to gallop away, followed by his attendant. At length he succeeded in reaching a priory, where he was received and protected from farther danger, having, in the mean time, given up the falcon. When the excitement had subsided he resumed his journey, and at length, without any farther adventures, reached the coast at the point nearest to Sicily. Here he passed the night in a tent, which he pitched upon the rocks on the shore, waiting for arrangements to be made on the next day for his public entrance into the harbor of Messina, which lay just opposite to him, across the narrow strait that here separates the island of Sicily from the main land.

[Pg 117]

Chapter VIII.

King Richard at Messina.

1190

The triumphal entry into Messina.
The jealousy of the Sicilians and the envy of the French.

Although Richard came down to the Italian shore, opposite to Messina, almost unattended and alone, and under circumstances so ignoble—fugitive as he was from a party of peasants whom he had incensed by an act of petty robbery—he yet made his entry at last into the town itself with a great display of pomp and parade. He remained on the Italian side of the strait, after he arrived on the shore, until he had sent over to Messina, and informed the officers of his fleet, which, by the way, had already arrived there, that he had come. The whole fleet immediately got ready, and came over to the Italian side to take Richard on board and escort him over. Richard entered the harbor with his fleet as if he were a conqueror returning home. The ships and galleys were all fully manned and gayly decorated, and Richard arranged such a number of musicians on the decks of them to blow trumpets and horns as the fleet sailed along the shores and [Pg 118] entered the harbor that the air was filled with the echoes of them, and the whole country was called out by the sound. The Sicilians were quite alarmed to see so formidable a host of foreign soldiers coming among them; and even their allies, the French, were not pleased. Philip began to be jealous of Richard's superior power, and to be alarmed at his assuming and arrogant demeanor. Philip had arrived in Messina some time before this, but his fleet, which was originally an inferior one, having consisted of such vessels only as he could hire at Genoa, had been greatly injured by storms during the passage, so that he had reached Messina in a very crippled condition. And now to see Richard coming in apparently so much his superior, and with so evident a disposition to make a parade of his superiority, made him anxious and uneasy.

The same feeling manifested itself, too, among his troops, and this to such a degree as to threaten to break out into open quarrels between the soldiers of the two armies.

"It will never answer," thought Philip, "for us both to remain long at Messina; so I will set out again myself as soon as I possibly can."

[Pg 119]

The winter sets in upon Richard and Philip in Sicily.

Indeed, there was another very decisive reason for Philip's soon continuing his voyage, and that was the necessity of diminishing the number of soldiers now at Messina on account of the difficulty of finding sustenance for them all. Philip accordingly made all haste to refit his fleet and to sail away; but he was again unfortunate. He encountered another storm, and was obliged to put back again, and before he could be ready a second time the winter set in, and he was obliged to give up all hope of leaving Sicily until the spring.

Winter quarters.

The two kings had foreseen this difficulty, and had earnestly endeavored to avoid it by making all their arrangements in the first instance for setting out from England and France in March, which was the earliest possible season for navigating the Mediterranean safely with such vessels as they had in those days. But this plan the reader will recollect had been frustrated by the death of Philip's queen, and the delays attendant upon that event, as well as other delays arising from other causes, and it was past midsummer before the expedition was ready to take its departure. The kings had still hoped to have reached the Holy Land before winter, but now they found themselves [Pg 120] stopped on the way, and Philip, with many misgivings in respect to the result, prepared to make the best arrangements that he could for putting his men into winter quarters.

Tancred.

Richard did in the end become involved in difficulties with Philip and with the French troops, but the most serious affair which occupied his attention was a very extraordinary quarrel which he instigated between himself and the king of the country. The name of this king was Tancred.

His history.

The kingdom of Sicily in those days included not merely the island of Sicily, but also nearly all the southern part of Italy — all that part, namely, which forms the foot and ankle of Italy, as seen upon the map. It has already been said that Richard's sister Joanna some years ago married the king of this country. The name of the king whom Joanna married was William, and he was now dead. Tancred was his successor, though not the regular and rightful heir. In order that the reader may understand the nature of the quarrel which broke out between Tancred and Richard, it is necessary to explain how it happened that Tancred succeeded to the throne.

William of Sicily.

If William, Joanna's husband, had had a [Pg 121] son, he would have been the rightful successor; but William had no children, and some time before his death he gave up all expectation of ever having any, so he began to look around and consider who should be his heir.

Constance.
Oath of allegiance.

He fixed his mind upon a lady, the Princess Constance, who was his cousin and his nearest relative. She would have been the heir had it not been that the usages of the realm did not allow a woman to reign. There was another relative of William, a young man named Tancred. For some reasons, William was very unwilling that Tancred should succeed him. He knew, however, that the people would be extremely averse to receive Constance as their sovereign instead of Tancred, on account of her being a woman; but he thought that he might obviate this objection in some degree by arranging a marriage for her with some powerful prince. This he finally succeeded in doing. The prince whom he chose was a son of the Emperor of Germany. His name was Henry. Constance was married to him, and after her marriage she left Sicily and went home with her husband. William then assembled all his barons, and made them take an oath of allegiance to Constance and Henry, as rightful sovereigns [Pg 122] after his decease. Supposing every thing to be thus amicably arranged, he settled himself quietly in his capital, the city of Palermo, intending to live there in peace with his wife for the remainder of his days.

Joanna's estates in the promontory of Mont Gargano.

When he married Joanna, he had given her, for her dower, a large territory of rich estates in Italy. These estates were all together, and comprised what is called the promontory of Mont Gargano. You will see this promontory represented on any map of Italy by a small projection on the heel, or, rather, a little way above the heel of the foot, on the eastern side of the peninsula. It is nearly opposite to Naples. This territory was large, and contained, besides a number of valuable landed estates, several castles, with lakes and forests adjoining; also two monasteries, with their pastures, woods, and vineyards, and several beautiful lakes. These estates, and all the income from them, were secured to Joanna forever.

Tancred seizing the power.

Not very long after William had completed his arrangements for the succession, he died unexpectedly, while Constance was away from the kingdom, at home with her husband. Immediately a great number of competitors started up and claimed the crown. Among them was [Pg 123] Tancred. Tancred took the field, and, after a desperate contest with his rivals, at length carried the day. He considered Joanna, the queen dowager, as his enemy, and either confiscated her estates or allowed others to seize them. He then took her with him to Palermo, where, as Richard was led to believe, he kept her a prisoner. All these things happened a few months only before Richard arrived in Messina.

A good pretext for war.

Palermo, as you will see from any map of Sicily, lies near the northwest corner of Sicily, and Messina near the northeast. In consequence of these occurrences, it happened that when Richard landed in Sicily he found his sister, the wife of the former king of the country, a widow and a prisoner, and her estates confiscated, while a person whom he considered a usurper was on the throne. A better state of things to furnish him with a pretext for aggressions on the country or the people he could not possibly have desired.

Richard's demand.
Tancred's response.

As soon as he had landed his troops, he formed a great encampment for them on the sea-shore, outside the town. The place of the encampment was bordered at one extremity by the suburbs of the town, and at the other extremity was a monastery built on a height. [Pg 124] As soon as Richard had established himself here, he sent a delegation to Tancred at Palermo, demanding that he should release Joanna and send her to him. Tancred denied that Joanna had been imprisoned at all, and, at any rate, he immediately acceded to her brother's demand that she should be sent to him. He placed her on board one of his own royal galleys, and caused her to be conveyed in it, with a very honorable escort, to Messina, and there delivered up to Richard's care.

In respect to the dower which Richard had demanded that he should restore, Tancred commenced giving some explanations in regard to it, but Richard was too impatient to listen to them. "We will not wait," said he to his sister, "to hear any talking on the subject; we will go and take possession of the territory ourselves."

Reprisals.
Fortifying a monastery.

So he embarked a part of his army on board some ships and transported them across the Straits, and, landing on the Italian shore, he seized a castle and a portion of territory surrounding it. He put a strong garrison in the castle, and gave the command of it to Joanna, while he went back to Messina to strengthen the position of the remainder of his army there. [Pg 125] He thought that the monastery which flanked his encampment on the side farthest from the town would make a good fortress if he had possession of it, and that, if well fortified, it would strengthen very much the defenses of his encampment in case Tancred should attempt to molest him. So he at once took possession of it. He turned the monks out of doors, removed all the sacred implements and emblems, and turned the buildings into a fortress. He put in a garrison of soldiers to guard it, and filled the rooms which the monks had been accustomed to use for their studies and their prayers with stores of arms and ammunition brought in from the ships, and with other apparatus of war. His object was to be ready to meet Tancred, at a moment's warning, if he should attempt to attack him.

Soldiers' troubles.
The army provokes a riot in Messina.

Soon after this a very serious difficulty broke out between the soldiers of the army and the people of Messina. There is almost always difficulty between the soldiers of an army and the people of any town near which the army is encamped. The soldiers, brutal in their passions, and standing in awe of none but their own officers, are often exceedingly violent and unjust in their demeanor toward unarmed and helpless [Pg 126] citizens, and the citizens, though they usually endure very long and very patiently, sometimes become aroused to resentment and retaliation at last. In this case, parties of Richard's soldiers went into Messina, and behaved so outrageously toward the inhabitants, and especially toward the young women, that the indignation of the husbands and fathers was excited to the highest degree. The soldiers were attacked in the streets. Several of them were killed. The rest fled, and were pursued by the crowd of citizens to the gates. Those that escaped went to the camp, breathless with excitement and burning with rage, and called upon all their fellow-soldiers to join them and revenge their wrongs. A great riot was created, and bands of furious men, hastily collected together, advanced toward the city, brandishing their arms and uttering furious cries, determined to break through the gates and kill every body that they could find. Richard heard of the danger just in time to mount his horse and ride to the gates of the city, and there to head off the soldiers and drive them back; but they were so furious that, for a time, they would not hear him, but still pressed on. He was obliged to ride in among them, and actually beat them back with [Pg 127] his truncheon, before he could compel them to give up their design.

The intense excitement.
The conference broken up.
Richard's uncontrollable passion.

The next day a meeting of the chief officers in the two armies, with the chief magistrates and some of the principal citizens of Messina, was held, to consider what to do to settle this dispute, and to prevent future outbreaks of this character. But the state of excitement between the two parties was too great to be settled yet in any amicable manner. While the conference was proceeding, a great crowd of people from the town collected on a rising ground just above the place where the conference was sitting. They said they only came as spectators. Richard alleged, on the other hand, that they were preparing to attack the conference. At any rate, they were excited and angry, and assumed a very threatening attitude. Some Normans who approached them got into an altercation with them, and at length one of the Normans was killed, and the rest cried out, "To arms!" The conference broke up in confusion. Richard rushed to the camp and called out his men. He was in a state of fury. Philip did all in his power to allay the storm and to prevent a combat, and when he found that Richard would not listen to him, he declared that he had [Pg 128] a great mind to join with the Sicilians and fight him. This, however, he did not do, but contented himself with doing all he could to calm the excitement of his angry ally. But Richard was not to be controlled. He rushed on, at the head of his troops, up the hill to the ground where the Sicilians were assembled. He attacked them furiously. They were, to some extent, armed, but they were not organized, and, of course, they could not stand against the charge of the soldiers. They fled in confusion toward the city. Richard and his troops followed them, killing as many of them as they could in the pursuit. The Sicilians crowded into the city and shut the gates. Of course, the whole town was now alarmed, and all the people that could fight were marshaled on the walls and at the gates to defend themselves.

The attack on Messina.

Richard retired for a brief period till he could bring on a larger force, and then made a grand attack on the walls. Several of his officers and soldiers were killed by darts and arrows from the battlements, but at length the walls were taken by storm, the gates were opened, and Richard marched in at the head of his troops. When the people were entirely subdued, Richard hung out his flag on a high tower in token [Pg 129] that he had taken full and formal possession of Tancred's capital.

Contest between Philip and Richard.

Philip remonstrated against this very strongly, but Richard declared that, now that he had got possession of Messina, he would keep possession until Tancred came to terms with him in respect to his sister Joanna. Philip insisted that he should not do this, but threatened to break off the alliance unless Richard would give up the town. Finally the matter was compromised by Richard agreeing that he would take down the flag and withdraw from the town himself, and for the present put it under the government of certain knights that he and Philip should jointly appoint for this purpose.

A reconciliation.

After the excitement of this affair had a little subsided, Richard and Philip began to consider how unwise it was for them to quarrel with each other, engaged as they were together in an enterprise of such magnitude and of so much hazard, and one in which it was impossible for them to hope to succeed, unless they continued united, and so they became reconciled, or, at least, pretended to be so, and made new vows of eternal friendship and brotherhood.

Fortifying.

Still, notwithstanding these protestations, Richard went on lording it over the Sicilians [Pg 130] in the most high-handed manner. Some nobles of high rank were so indignant at these proceedings that they left the town. Richard immediately confiscated their estates and converted the proceeds to his own use. He proceeded to fortify his encampment more and more. The monastery which he had forcibly taken from the monks he turned into a complete castle. He made battlements on the walls, and surrounded the whole with a moat. He also built another castle on the hills commanding the town. He acted, in a word, in all respects as if he considered himself master of the country. He did not consult Philip at all in respect to any of these proceedings, and he paid no attention to the remonstrances that Philip from time to time addressed to him. Philip was exceedingly angry, but he did not see what he could do.

Richard brings Tancred to terms.
What Richard required of Tancred.

Tancred, too, began to be very much alarmed. He wished to know of Richard what it was that he demanded in respect to Joanna. Richard said he would consider and let him know. In a short time he made known his terms as follows. He said that Tancred must restore to his sister all the territories which, as he alleged, had belonged to her, and also give her "a golden chair, a golden table twelve feet [Pg 131] long and a foot and a half broad, two golden supports for the same, four silver cups, and four silver dishes." He pretended that, by a custom of the realm, she was entitled to these things. He also demanded for himself a very large contribution toward the armament and equipment for the crusade. It seems that at one period during the lifetime of William, Joanna's husband, her father, King Henry of England, was planning a crusade, and that William, by a will which he made at that time—so at least Richard maintained—had bequeathed a large contribution toward the necessary means for fitting it out. The items were these:

1. Sixty thousand measures of wheat.

2. The same quantity of barley.

3. A fleet of a thousand armed galleys, equipped and provisioned for two years.

4. A silken tent large enough to accommodate two hundred knights sitting at a banquet.

These particulars show on how great a scale these military expeditions for conquering the Holy Land were conducted in those days, the above list being only a complimentary contribution to one of them by a friend of the leader of it.

Richard now maintained that, though his father [Pg 132] Henry had died without going on the crusade, still he himself was going, and that he, being the son, and consequently the representative and heir of Henry, was, as such, entitled to receive the bequest; so he called upon Tancred to pay it.

The final conditions of peace.

After much negotiation, the dispute was settled by Richard's waiving these claims, and arranging the matter on a new and different basis. He had a nephew named Arthur. Arthur was yet very young, being only about two years old; and as Richard had no children of his own, Arthur was his presumptive heir. Tancred had a daughter, yet an infant. Now it was finally proposed that Arthur and this young daughter of Tancred should be affianced, and that Tancred should pay to Richard twenty thousand pieces of gold as her dowry! Richard was, of course, to take this money as the guardian and trustee of his nephew, and he was to engage that, if any thing should occur hereafter to prevent the marriage from taking place, he would refund the money. Tancred was also to pay Richard twenty thousand pieces of gold besides, in full settlement of all claims in behalf of Joanna. These terms were finally agreed to on both sides.

[Pg 133]

King Richard's league with Tancred.

Richard also entered into a league, offensive and defensive, with Tancred, agreeing to assist him in maintaining his position as King of Sicily against all his enemies. This is a very important circumstance to be remembered, for the chief of Tancred's enemies was the Emperor Henry of Germany, the prince who had married Constance, as has been already related. Henry's father had died, and he had become Emperor of Germany himself, and he now claimed Sicily as the inheritance of Constance his wife, according to the will of King William, Joanna's husband. Tancred, he maintained, was a usurper, and, of course, now Richard, by his league, offensive and defensive, with Tancred, made himself Henry's enemy. This led him into serious difficulty with Henry at a subsequent period, as we shall by-and-by see.

The treaty signed.
Royal trustees are not always faithful.

The treaty between Richard and Tancred was drawn up in due form and duly executed, and it was sent for safe keeping to Rome, and there deposited with the Pope. Tancred paid Richard the money, and he immediately began to squander it in the most lavish and extravagant manner. He expended the infant princess's dower, which he held in trust for Arthur, as freely as he did the other money. Indeed, this [Pg 134] was a very common way, in those days, for great kings to raise money. If they had a young son or heir, no matter how young he was, they would contract to give him in marriage to the little daughter of some other potentate on condition of receiving some town, or castle, or province, or large sum of money as dower. The idea was, of course, that they were to take this dower in charge for the young prince, to keep it for him until he should become old enough to be actually married, but in reality they would take possession of the property themselves, and convert it at once to their own use.

Richard himself had been affianced in this way in his infancy to Alice, the daughter of the then reigning King of France, and the sister of Philip, and his father, King Henry the Second, had received and appropriated the dowry.

Extravagance of Richard's court.

Indeed, in this case, both the sums of money that Richard received from Tancred were paid to Richard in trust, or, at least, ought to have been so regarded, the one amount being for Arthur, and the other for Joanna. Richard himself, in his own name, had no claims on Tancred whatever; but as soon as the money came into his hands, he began to expend it in the most profuse and lavish manner. He adopted [Pg 135] a very extravagant and ostentatious style of living. He made costly presents to the barons, and knights, and officers of the armies, including the French army as well as his own, and gave them most magnificent entertainments. Philip thought that he did this to secure popularity, and that the presents which he made to the French knights and nobles were designed to entice them away from their allegiance and fidelity to him, their lawful sovereign. At Christmas he gave a splendid entertainment, to which he invited every person of the rank of a knight or a gentleman in both armies, and at the close of the feast he made a donation in money to each of the guests, the sum being different in different cases, according to the rank and station of the person who received it.

Spring approaching.
Repairing the fleet.
Battering-rams.

The king, having thus at last settled his quarrels and established himself in something like peace in Sicily, began to turn his attention toward the preparations for the spring. Of course, his intention was, as soon as the spring should open, to set sail with his fleet and army, and proceed toward the Holy Land. He now caused all his ships to be examined with a view to ascertain what repairs they needed. Some had been injured by the storms which they had [Pg 136] encountered on the way from Marseilles or by accidents of the sea. Others had become worm-eaten and leaky by lying in port. Richard caused them all to be put thoroughly in repair. He also caused a number of battering engines to be constructed of timber which his men hauled from the forests around the base of Mount Ætna. These engines were for assailing the walls of the towns and fortresses in the Holy Land.

Modern ordnance.

In modern times walls are always attacked with mortars and cannon. The ordnance of the present day will throw shot and shells of prodigious weight two or three miles, and these tremendous missiles strike against the walls of a fortress with such force as in a short time to batter them down, no matter how strong and thick they may be. But in those days gunpowder was not in use, and the principal means of breaking down a wall was by the battering-ram, which consisted of a heavy beam of wood, hung by a rope or chain from a massive frame, and then swung against the gate or wall which it was intended to break through. In the engraving you see such a ram suspended from the frame, with men at work below, impelling it against a gateway.

[Pg 137-8]

THE BATTERING-RAM.

[Pg 139]

The methods of war in ancient times.

Sometimes these battering-rams were very large and heavy, and the men drew them back and forth, in striking the wall with them, by means of ropes. There are accounts of some battering-rams which weighed forty or fifty tons, and required fifteen hundred men to work them.

The men, of course, were very much exposed while engaged in this operation, for the people whom they were besieging would gather on the walls above, and shoot spears, darts, and arrows at them, and throw down stones and other missiles, as you see in the engraving.

THE BALLISTA.
Catapultas.
Ballistas.
Maginalls.

Then, besides the battering-ram, which, though very efficient against walls, was of no service against men, there were other engines [Pg 140] made in those days which were designed to throw stones or monstrous darts. These last were, of course, designed to operate against bodies of men. They were made in various forms, and were called catapultas, ballistas, maginalls, and by other such names. The force with which they operated consisted of springs made by elastic bars of wood, twisted ropes, and other such contrivances.

THE CATAPULTA.

Some were for throwing stones, others for monstrous darts. Of course, these engines required for their construction heavy frames of sound timber. Richard did not expect to find such timber in the Holy Land, nor did he wish [Pg 141] to consume the time after he should arrive in making them; so he employed the winter in constructing a great number of these engines, and in packing them, in parts, on board his galleys.

The religious observances of tyrants.

Richard performed a great religious ceremony, too, while he was at Sicily this winter, as a part of the preparation which he deemed it necessary to make for the campaign. It is a remarkable fact that every great military freebooter that has organized an armed gang of men to go forth, and rob and murder his fellow-men, in any age of the world, has considered some great religious performance necessary at the outset of the work, to prepare the minds of his soldiers for it, and to give them the necessary resolution and confidence in it. It was so with Alexander. It was so with Xerxes and with Darius. It was so with Pyrrhus. It is so substantially at the present day, when, in all wars, each side makes itself the champion of heaven in the contest, and causes Te Deums to be chanted in their respective churches, now on this side and now on that, in pretended gratitude to God for their alternate victories.

Richard's penitence and penance.

Richard called a grand convention of all the prelates and monks that were with his army, [Pg 142] and performed a solemn act of worship. A part of the performance consisted of his kneeling personally before the priests, confessing his sins and the wicked life that he had led, and making very fervent promises to sin no more, and then, after submitting to the penances which they enjoined upon him, receiving from them pardon and absolution. After the enactment of this solemnity, the soldiers felt far more safe and strong in going forth to the work which lay before them in the Holy Land than before.

Was he sincere?

Nor is it certain that in this act Richard was wholly hypocritical and insincere. The human heart is a mansion of many chambers, and a religious sentiment, in no small degree conscientious and honest, though hollow and mistaken, may have strong possession of some of them, while others are filled to overflowing with the dear and besetting sins, whatever they are, by which the general conduct of the man is controlled.

[Pg 143]

Chapter IX.

Berengaria.

1190

Richard's betrothal to Berengaria.

W hile Richard was in the kingdom of Sicily during this memorable winter, he made a new contract of marriage. The lady was a Spanish princess named Berengaria. The circumstances of this betrothment were somewhat extraordinary.

The obstacles which prevented the marriage of Richard and Alice.

The reader will recollect that he had been betrothed in his earliest youth to Alice, an infant princess of France. His father had thrown him in, as it were, as a sort of makeweight, in arranging some compromise with the King of France for the settlement of a quarrel, and also to obtain the dower of the young princess for his own use. This dower consisted of various castles and estates, which were immediately put into the hands of Henry, Richard's father, and which he continued to hold as long as he lived, using and enjoying the rents and revenues from them as his own property. When Richard grew old enough to claim his bride, Henry, under whose custody and charge she had been [Pg 144] placed, would not give her up to him; and long and serious quarrels arose between the father and the son on this account, as has already been related in this volume. The most obvious reason for which Henry might be supposed unwilling to give up Alice to her affianced husband, when he became old enough to be married to her, was, that he wished to retain longer the use of the castles and estates that constituted her dowry. But, in addition to this, it was surmised by many that he had actually fallen in love with her himself, and that he was determined that Richard should not have her at all. Richard himself believed, or pretended to believe, that this was the case. He was consequently very angry, and he justified himself in the wars and rebellions that he raised against his father during the lifetime of the king by this great wrong which he alleged that his father had done him. On the other hand, many persons supposed that Richard did not really wish to marry Alice, and that he only made the fact of his father's withholding her from him a pretext for his unnatural hostility, the real ends and aims of which were objects altogether different.

However this may be, when Henry died, and [Pg 145] there was no longer any thing in the way of his marriage, he showed no desire to consummate it. Alice's father, too, had died, and Philip, the present King of France, and Richard's ally, was her brother. Philip called upon Richard from time to time to complete the marriage, but Richard found various pretexts for postponing it, and thus the matter stood when the expedition for the Holy Land set sail from Marseilles.

The first acquaintance of Richard and the Princess Berengaria.

The next reason why Richard did not now wish to carry his marriage with Alice into effect was that, in the mean time, while his father had been withholding Alice from him, he had seen and fallen in love with another lady, the Princess Berengaria. Richard first saw Berengaria several years before, at a time when he was with his mother in Aquitaine, during the life of his father. The first time that he saw her was at a grand tournament which was celebrated in her native city in Spain, and which Richard went to attend. The families had been well acquainted with each other before, though, until the tournament, Richard had never seen Berengaria. Richard had, however, known one of her brothers from his boyhood, and they had always been very great friends. The father of Berengaria, too, Sancho the Wise, King of Navarre, had always [Pg 146] been a warm friend of Eleanora, Richard's mother, and in the course of the difficulties and quarrels that took place between her and her husband, as related in the early chapters of this volume, he had rendered her very valuable services. Still, Richard never saw Berengaria until she had grown up to womanhood.

The fame of Berengaria.
Her accomplishments.

He, however, felt a strong desire to see her, for she was quite celebrated for her beauty and her accomplishments. The accomplishments in which she excelled were chiefly music and poetry. Richard himself was greatly interested in these arts, especially in the songs of the Troubadours, whose performances always formed a very important part of the entertainment at the feasts and tournaments, and other great public celebrations of those days.

When Richard came to see Berengaria, he fell deeply in love with her. But he could not seek her hand in marriage on account of his engagement with Alice. To have given up Alice, and to have entered instead into an engagement with her, would have involved both him and his mother, and all the family of Berengaria too, in a fierce quarrel with the King of France, the father of Alice, and also with his own father. These were too serious consequences [Pg 147] for him to brave while he was still only a prince, and nominally under his father's authority. So he did nothing openly, though a strong secret attachment sprang up between him and Berengaria, and all desire ever to make Alice his wife gradually disappeared.

Eleanora sent to King Sancho to ask his daughter in marriage.

At length, when his father died, and Richard became King of England, he felt at once that the power was now in his own hands, and that he would do as he liked in respect to his marriage. Alice's father, too, had died, and her brother Philip was now king, and he was not likely to feel so strong an interest in resenting any supposed slight to his sister as her father would have been. Richard determined, therefore, to give up Alice altogether, and ask Berengaria to be his wife. So, while he was engaged in England in making his preparations for the crusade, and when he was nearly ready to set out, he sent his mother, Eleanora, to Navarre to ask Berengaria in marriage of her father, King Sancho. He did not, however, give Philip any notice of this change in his plans, not wishing to embarrass the alliance that he and Philip were forming with any unnecessary difficulties which might interfere with the success of it, and retard the preparations for the crusade. [Pg 148] So, while his mother had gone to Spain to secure Berengaria for him as his wife, he himself, in England and Normandy, went on with his preparations for the crusade in connection with Philip, just as if the original engagement with Alice was going regularly on.

Berengaria's acceptance.

Eleanora was very successful in her mission. Sancho, Berengaria's father, was very much pleased with so magnificent an offer as that of the hand of Richard, Duke of Normandy and King of England, for his daughter. Berengaria herself made no objection. Eleanora said that her son had not been able to come himself and claim his bride, on account of the necessity that he was under of accompanying his army to the East, but she said that he would stop at Messina, and she proposed that Berengaria should put herself under her protection, and go and join him there.

The expedition to meet Richard.

Berengaria was a lady of an ardent and romantic temperament, and nothing could please her better than such a proposal as this. She very readily acceded to it, and her father was very willing to intrust her to the charge of Eleanora. So the two ladies, with a proper train of barons, knights, and other attendants, set out together. They crossed the Pyrenees into [Pg 149] France, and then, after traversing France, they passed over the Alps into Italy. Thence they continued their journey down the Italian coast by land, as Richard had done by water, until at last they arrived at a place called Brindisi, which is on the coast of Italy, not far from Messina. Here they halted, and sent word to Richard to inform him of their arrival.

Eleanora thought that Berengaria could not go any farther with propriety, for her engagement with Richard was not yet made public. Indeed, the betrothal of Richard with Alice still remained nominally in force, and a serious difficulty was to be apprehended with Philip so soon as the new plans which Richard had formed should be announced to him.

Berengaria at Brindisi with Joanna.
The friendship between Joanna and Berengaria.

Eleanora said that she could not remain long in Italy, but must return to Normandy very soon, without waiting for Richard to prepare the way for receiving his bride. So she left Berengaria under the charge of Joanna, who, being her own—that is, Eleanora's—daughter, was a very proper person to be the young lady's protector. Joanna and Berengaria immediately conceived a strong attachment for each other, and they lived together in a very happy manner. Joanna was glad to have for a companion [Pg 150] so charming a young lady, and one of so high a rank, and Berengaria, on the other hand, was much pleased to be placed under the charge of so kind a protector. Joanna, too, having long lived in Sicily, could give Berengaria a great deal of interesting intelligence about the country and the people, and could answer all the thousand questions which she asked about what she heard and saw in the new world, as it were, into which she had been ushered.

The two ladies lived, of course, in very close seclusion, but they lived so lovingly together that one of the writers of the day, in a ballad that he wrote, compared them to two birds in a cage. Speaking of Eleanora, he says, in the quaint old English of the day,

> "She beleft Berengere At Richard's costage. Queen Joanne held her dear; They lived as doves in a cage."

The arrival of Berengaria at Brindisi took place in the spring of the year, when the time was drawing nigh for the fleets and armaments to sail for the East. As yet, Philip knew nothing of Richard's plans in respect to this new marriage, but the time had now arrived when Richard perceived that they could no longer be [Pg 151] concealed. Philip entertained suspicions that something wrong was going on, though he did not know exactly what. His suspicions made him watchful and jealous, and at last they led to a curious train of circumstances, which brought matters to a crisis very suddenly.

Tancred receives a letter from Philip.
Treachery.

It seems that at one time, when Richard was paying a visit to Tancred, the King of Sicily, Tancred showed him a letter which he said he had received from the French king. In this letter, Philip—if, indeed, Philip really wrote it—endeavored to excite Tancred's enmity against Richard. It was just after the treaty between Tancred and Richard had been formed, as related in the last chapter. The letter said that Richard was a treacherous man, in whom no reliance could be placed; that he had no intention of keeping the treaty that he had made, but was laying a scheme for attacking Tancred in his Sicilian dominions; and, finally, it closed with an offer on the part of the writer to assist Tancred in driving Richard and all his followers out of the island.

[Pg 152]

THE LETTER.
Philip's letter to Tancred.
Richard's opinion of it.

When Richard read this letter, he was at first in a dreadful rage, and he broke out into an explosion of the most violent, profane, and passionate language that can be conceived. Presently he looked at the letter again, and on reperusing it, and carefully considering its contents, he declared that he did not believe that Philip ever wrote it. It was a stratagem of Tancred's, he thought, designed to promote a quarrel between Richard and his ally. Tancred assured him that Philip did write the letter, or, at least, that it was brought to him as [Pg 153] from Philip by the Duke of Burgundy, one of his principal officers.

"You may ask the Duke of Burgundy," said he, "and if he denies it, I will challenge him to a duel through one of my barons."

The etiquette of dueling.

It was necessary that the parties to a duel, in those days, should be of equal rank, so that, if a king had a quarrel with a nobleman of another nation, he could only send one of his own noblemen of the same rank to be his representative in the combat. But this proposal of sending another man to risk his life in maintaining the cause of his king on a question of veracity, in which the person so sent had no interest whatever, illustrates very curiously the ideas of those chivalrous times.

Richard charges the letter upon Philip.

Richard did not go to the Duke of Burgundy, but, taking the letter which Tancred had shown him, he waited until he found a good opportunity, and then showed it to Philip. The two kings often fell into altercations and disputes in their interviews with each other, and it was in one of these that Richard produced the letter, offering it by way of recrimination to some charges or accusations which Philip was making against him. Philip denied having written the letter. It was a forgery, he said, and [Pg 154] he believed that Richard himself was the author of it.

Philip's reply.

"You are trying every way you can," said he, "to find pretexts for quarreling with me, and this is one of your devices. I know what you are aiming at: you wish to quarrel with me so as to find some excuse for breaking off your marriage with my sister, whom you are bound by a most solemn oath to marry. But of this you may be sure, that if you abandon her and take any other wife, you will find me, as long as you live, your most determined and mortal enemy."

This declaration aroused Richard's temper, and brought the affair at once to a crisis. Richard declared to Philip that he never would marry his sister.

Richard's declaration.

"My father," said he, "kept her from me for many years because he loved her himself, and she returned his love, and now I will never have any thing to do with her. I am ready to prove to you the truth of what I say."

So Richard brought forward what he called the proofs of the very intimate relations which had subsisted between Alice and his father. Whether there was any thing genuine or conclusive in these proofs is not known. At all [Pg 155] events, they made a very deep and painful impression on Philip. The disclosure was, as one of the writers of those times says, "like a nail driven directly through his heart."

Richard and Philip compromise their quarrel.

After a while, the two kings concluded to settle the difficulty by a sort of compromise. Philip agreed to give up all claims on the part of Alice to Richard in consideration of a sum of money which Richard was to pay. Richard was to pay two thousand marks [D] a year for five years, and was on that condition to be allowed to marry any one he chose. He was also to restore to Philip the fortresses and estates which had been conveyed to his father as Alice's dowry at the time of her betrothment to Richard in her infancy.

This agreement, being thus made, was confirmed by a great profusion of oaths, sworn with all solemnity, and the affair was considered as settled.

Re-embarkation.

Still, Richard seems to have been a little disinclined to bring out Berengaria at once from her retreat, and let Philip know suddenly how far his arrangements for marrying another lady had gone; so he concluded to wait, before publicly announcing his intended marriage, until [Pg 156] Philip should have sailed for the East. Philip was now, indeed, nearly ready to go; his fleet and his armament, being smaller than Richard's, could be dispatched earlier; so Richard devoted himself very earnestly to the work of facilitating and hastening his ally's departure, determining that immediately afterward he would bring forward his bride and celebrate his marriage.

Preparations for the marriage.

It is not, however, certain that he kept his intended marriage with Berengaria an absolute secret from Philip. There would be no longer any special necessity for this after the treaty that had been made. But, notwithstanding this agreement, it is not to be supposed that the new marriage would be a very agreeable subject for Philip to contemplate, or that it would be otherwise than very awkward for him to be present on the occasion of the celebration of it; so Richard decided that, on all accounts, it was best to postpone the ceremony until after Philip had gone.

Richard escorting Philip.

Philip sailed the very last of March. Richard selected from his fleet a few of his most splendid galleys, and with these, filled with a chosen company of knights and barons, he accompanied Philip as he left the harbor, and [Pg 157] sailed with him down the Straits of Messina, with trumpets sounding, and flags and banners waving in the air. As soon as Philip's fleet reached the open sea, Richard took leave, and set out with his galleys on his return; but, instead of going back to Messina, he made the best of his way to the port in Italy where Berengaria and Joanna were lodging, and there took the ladies, who were all ready, expecting him, and embarking them on board a very elegantly adorned galley which he had prepared for them, he conducted them to Messina.

Why the wedding was postponed.

Richard would now probably have been immediately married, but it was in the season of Lent, and, according to the ideas of those times, it would be in some sense a desecration of that holy season of fasting to celebrate any such joyous ceremony as a wedding in it; and it would not do very well to postpone the sailing of the fleet until after the season of Lent should have expired, for the time had already fully arrived when it ought to sail, and Philip, with his division of the allied force, had already gone; so he concluded to put off his marriage till they should reach the next place at which the expedition should land.

Berengaria consented to this, and it was arranged [Pg 158] that she was to accompany the expedition when it should sail, and that at the next place of landing, which it was expected would be the island of Rhodes, the marriage ceremony should be performed.

Richard puts Joanna and Berengaria in charge of Stephen.

As it was not considered quite proper, however, under these circumstances, that the princess should sail in the same ship with Richard, a very strong and excellent ship was provided for her special use, and that of Joanna who was to accompany her, and it was arranged that she should sail from the port just before the main body of the fleet were ready to commence the voyage. The ship in which the ladies and their suite were conveyed was placed under the command of a brave and faithful knight named Stephen of Turnham, and the two princesses were committed to his special charge.

The vow to conquer Acre.

But, although Richard's regard for the sacred season of Lent would not allow of his celebrating the marriage, he made a grand celebration in honor of his betrothment to Berengaria before he sailed. At this celebration he instituted an order of twenty-four knights. These knights bound themselves in a fraternity with the king, and took a solemn oath that they would scale the walls of Acre when they reached [Pg 159] the Holy Land. Acre was one of the strongest and most important fortresses in that country, and one which they were intending first to attack.

Richard's present to Tancred.

Also, before he went away, Richard made King Tancred a farewell present of a very valuable antique sword, which had been found, he said, by his father in the tomb of a famous old English knight who had lived some centuries before.

[Pg 160]

Chapter X.

The Campaign in Cyprus.

1190

The expedition is at last ready to sail from Sicily.

T he time at length fully arrived for the departure of the English fleet from Sicily for the purpose of continuing the voyage to the Holy Land. Besides the delay which had been occasioned to Richard by circumstances connected with his marriage, he had waited also a short time for some store-ships to arrive from England with ammunition and supplies. When the store-ships at length came, the day for the sailing was immediately appointed, the tents were struck, the encampment abandoned, and the troops embarked on board the ships of the fleet.

The grand spectacle of the embarkation at Messina.

The Sicilians were all greatly excited, as the sailing of the fleet drew nigh, with anticipations of the splendor of the spectacle. The harbor was filled with ships of every form and size, and the movements connected with the embarkation of the troops on board of them, the striking of the tents, the packing up of furniture and goods, the hurrying of men to and fro, the crowding [Pg 161] at the landings, the rapid transit of boats back and forth between the ships and the shore, and all the other scenes and incidents usually attendant on the embarkation of a great army, occupied the attention of the people of the country, and filled them with excitement and pleasure. It is highly probable, too, that their pleasure was increased by the prospect that they were soon to be relieved from the presence of such troublesome and unmanageable visitors.

The order of sailing.

Never was a finer spectacle witnessed than that which was displayed by the sailing of the fleet, when the day for the departure of it at length arrived. The squadron consisted of nearly two hundred vessels in all. There were thirteen great ships, corresponding to what are called ships of the line of modern times. Then there were over fifty galleys. These were constructed so as to be propelled either by oars or by sails. Of course, when the wind was favorable, the sails would be used; but in case of calms, or of adverse winds blowing off from the land when the vessels were entering port, or of currents drifting them into danger, then the oars could be brought into requisition. In addition to these ships and galleys, there were about a hundred vessels used as transports for [Pg 162] the conveyance of provisions, stores, tents, and tent equipage, ammunition of all kinds, including the frames of the military engines which Richard had caused to be constructed in Sicily, and all the other supplies required for the use of a great army. Besides these there were a great many other smaller vessels, which were used as tenders, lighters, and for other such purposes, making a total number of nearly two hundred. In the order of sailing, the transports followed the ships and galleys, which were more properly the ships of war, and which led the van, in order the better to meet any danger which might appear, and the more effectually to protect the convoy from it.

Trenc-le-mer.

Richard sailed at the head of his fleet in a splendid galley, which was appropriated to his special use. The name of it was the Sea Cutter. [E] There was a huge lantern hoisted in the stern of Richard's galley, in order that the rest of the fleet could see and follow her in the night.

[Pg 163-4]

MAP
Illustrating the history of
KING RICHARD'S
CRUSADE.

The storm.
Navigation in the twelfth century.

The day of sailing was very fine, and the spectacle, witnessed by the Sicilians on shore, who watched the progress of it from every projecting point and headland as it moved majestically out of the harbor, was extremely grand. [Pg 165] For some time the voyage went on very prosperously, but at length the sky gradually became overcast, and the wind began to blow, and finally a great storm came on before the ships had time to seek any shelter. In those days there was no mariner's compass, and of course, in a storm, when the sun and stars were concealed, there was nothing to be done but for the ship to grope her way through the haze and rain for any land which might be near. The violence of the wind and the raging of the sea was in this case so great that the fleet was soon dispersed, and the vessels were driven northward and eastward toward certain islands which lie in that part of the Mediterranean, off the coasts of Asia Minor. The three principal of these islands, as you will see by the opposite map, are Candia, Rhodes, and Cyprus, Cyprus lying farther toward the east.

Limesol in Cyprus.
The wrecked ships.
King Richard's seal.

The ships came very near being wrecked on the coast of Crete, but they escaped and were driven onward over the sea, until at length a large portion of them found refuge at Rhodes. Others were driven on toward Cyprus. Richard's galley was among those that found refuge at Rhodes; but, unfortunately, the one in which Berengaria and Joanna were borne did not succeed [Pg 166] in making a port there, but was swept onward by the gale, and, in company with one or two others, was driven to the mouth of the harbor of Limesol, which is the principal port of Cyprus, and is situated on the south side of the island. The galley in which the queen and the princess were embarked, being probably of superior construction to the others, and better manned, succeeded in weathering the point and getting round into the harbor, but two or three other galleys which were with them struck and were wrecked. One of these ships was a very important one. It contained the chancellor who bore Richard's great seal, besides a number of other knights and crusaders of high rank, and many valuable goods. The seal was an object of great value. Every king had his own seal, which was used to authenticate his public acts. The one which belonged to Richard is represented in the following engraving.

The wreckers.
Isaac Comnenus.

As soon as the news of these wrecks spread into the island, the people came down in great numbers, and took possession of every thing of value which was cast upon the shore as property forfeited to the king of the country. The name of this king was Isaac Comnenus.

Law and justice.

He claimed that all wrecks cast upon his [Pg 167] shores were his property. That was the law of the land; it was, in fact, the law of a great many countries in those days, especially of such as had maritime coasts bordering on navigable waters that were specially exposed to storms.

Law is not the creator, but the protector of property.

Thus, in seizing the wreck of Richard's vessels, King Isaac had the law on his side, and all those who, in their theory of government, hold it as a principle that law is the foundation of property, and that what the law makes right is right, must admit that he had justice on his [Pg 168] side too. For my part, it seems clear that the right of property is anterior to all law, and independent of it. I think that the province of law is not to create property, but to protect it, and that it may, instead of protecting it, become the greatest violator of it. This law providing for the confiscation of property cast in wrecks upon a shore, and its forfeiture to the sovereign of the territory, is one of the most striking instances of aggression made by law on the natural and indefeasible rights of man.

In regard to the galley which contained the queens, that having escaped shipwreck, and having safely anchored in the harbor, the king had no pretext for molesting it in any way. He learned by some means that Queen Joanna was on board the galley; so he sent two boats down with a messenger, to inquire whether her majesty would be pleased to land.

Joanna's inquiries for her brother.

Stephen of Turnham, the knight who had command of the queen's galley, thought it not safe to go on shore, for by doing so Joanna and Berengaria would put themselves entirely in King Isaac's power; and though it was true that Isaac and the people of Cyprus over whom he ruled were Christians, yet they were of the Greek Church, while Richard and the English [Pg 169] were Roman, and these two churches were almost as hostile to each other as the Christians and the Turks. Stephen, however, communicated the message from Isaac to Joanna, and asked her majesty's pleasure thereupon. She sent back word to the messengers that she did not wish to land. She had only come into the harbor, she said, to see if she could learn any tidings of her brother; she had been separated from him by a great storm at sea, which had broken up and dispersed the fleet, and she wished to know whether any thing had been seen of him, or of any of his vessels, from the shores of that island.

An alarm.
A retreat.

The messengers replied that they did not know any thing about it, and so the boats returned back to the town. Soon after this the company on board the galley saw some armed vessels coming down the harbor toward them. They were alarmed at this sight, and immediately got every thing ready for setting off at a moment's notice to withdraw from the harbor. It turned out that the king himself was on board one of the galleys that was coming down, and this vessel was allowed to come near enough for the king to communicate with the people on board Joanna's galley. After some ordinary [Pg 170] questions had been asked and answered, the king, observing that a lady of high rank was standing on the deck with Joanna, asked who it was. They answered that it was the Princess of Navarre, who was going to be married to Richard. In the reply which the king made to this intelligence Stephen of Turnham thought he saw such indications of hostility that he deemed it most prudent to retire; so the anchor was raised, and the order was given to the oarsmen, who had already been stationed at their oars, to "give way," and the oarsmen pulled vigorously at the oars. The galley was immediately taken out into the offing. The King of Cyprus did not pursue her; so she anchored there quietly, the storm having now nearly subsided. Stephen resolved to wait there for a time, hoping that in some way or other he might soon receive intelligence from Richard.

Richard's vessel appears.
Richard's indignation on meeting Joanna's vessel.

Nor was he disappointed. Richard, whose galley, together with the principal portion of the fleet, had been driven farther to the eastward, had found refuge at Rhodes, and he set off, as soon as the storm abated, in pursuit of the missing vessels. He took with him a sufficient force to render to the vessels, if he should find them, such assistance or protection as might [Pg 171] be necessary. At length he reached Cyprus, and, on entering the bay, there he beheld the galley of Joanna and Berengaria riding safely at anchor in the offing. The sea had not yet gone down, and the vessel was rolling and tossing on the waves in a fearful manner. Richard was greatly enraged at beholding this spectacle, for he at once inferred, by seeing the vessel in this uncomfortable situation outside the harbor, that some difficulty with the authorities had occurred which prevented her seeking refuge and protection within. Accordingly, as soon as he came near, he leaped into a boat, although burdened as he was with heavy armor of steel, which was a difficult and somewhat dangerous operation, and ordered himself to be rowed immediately on board.

When he arrived, after the first greetings were over, he was informed by Stephen that three of the vessels of his fleet had been wrecked on the coast; that Isaac, the king, had seized them as his lawful prize; and that, at that very time, men that he had sent for this purpose were plundering the wrecks. Stephen also said that he had at first gone into the harbor with his galley, but that the indications of an unfriendly feeling on the part of the king were so [Pg 172] decided that he did not dare to stay, and he had been compelled to come out into the offing.

Richard's contest with King Isaac Comnenus.

On hearing these things Richard was greatly enraged. He sent a messenger on shore to the king to demand peremptorily that he should at once leave off plundering the wrecks of the English ships, and that he should deliver up to Richard again all the goods that had already been taken. To this demand Isaac replied that whatever goods the sea cast upon the shores of his island were his property, according to the law of the land, and that he should take them without asking leave of any body.

When Richard heard this answer, he was rather pleased than displeased with it, for it gave him, what he always wanted wherever he went, a pretext for quarreling. He said that the goods which Isaac obtained in that way he would find would cost him pretty dear, and he immediately prepared for war.

The history of the law of wrecks.

In this transaction there is no question that the King of Cyprus, though wholly wrong, and guilty of a real and inexcusable violation of the rights of property, had yet the law on his side. It was one of those cases, of which innumerable examples have existed in all ages of the world, where an act which is virtually the robbing [Pg 173] of one man by another is authorized by law, and is protected by legal sanctions. This rule — confiscating property wrecked — was the general law of Europe at this time, and Richard, of all men, might have considered himself estopped from objecting to it by the fact that it was the law in England as well as every where else. By the ancient common law of England, all wrecks of every kind became the property of the king. The severity of the rule had been slightly mitigated a few reigns before Richard's day by a statute which declared that if any living thing escaped from the wreck, even were it so much as a dog or a cat, that circumstance saved the property from confiscation, and preserved the claim of the owner to it. With this modification, the law stood in England until a very late period, that all goods thrown from wrecks upon the shores became the property of the crown, and it was not until comparatively quite a recent period that an English judge decided that such a principle, being contrary to justice and common sense, was not law; and now wrecked property is restored to whomsoever can prove himself to be the owner, on his paying for the expense and trouble of saving it.

Richard having landed, Isaac asks a truce.

On receiving the demand which Richard sent him, the King of Cyprus, anticipating difficulty, drew up his galleys in order of battle across the harbor, and marched troops down to commanding positions on the shore, wherever he thought there might be any danger that Richard would attempt to land. Richard very soon brought up his forces and advanced to attack him. Isaac's troops retreated as Richard advanced. Finally they were driven back without much actual contest into the town, and Richard then brought his squadron up into harbor and landed. Isaac, seeing how much stronger Richard was than he, did not attempt any serious resistance, but retired to the citadel. From the citadel he sent out a flag of truce demanding a parley.

Negotiating.

Richard granted the request, and an interview took place, but it led to no result. Richard found that Isaac was not yet absolutely subdued. He still asserted his rights, and complained of the gross wrong which Richard was perpetrating in invading his dominions, and seeking a quarrel with him without cause; but the effect was like that of the lamb attempting to resist or recriminate the wolf, which, far from bringing the aggressor to reason, only awakens [Pg 175] more strongly his ferocity and rage. Richard turned toward his attendants, and, uttering a profane exclamation, said that Isaac talked like a fool of a Briton.

Richard was a Norman, not an Englishman.

It is mentioned as a remarkable circumstance by the historians that Richard spoke these words in English, and it is said that this was the only time in the course of his life that he ever used that language. It may seem very strange to the reader that an English king should not ordinarily use the English language. But, strictly speaking, Richard was not an English king. He was a Norman king. The whole dynasty to which he belonged were Norman French in all their relations. Normandy they regarded as the chief seat of their empire. There were their principal cities—there their most splendid palaces. There they lived and reigned, with occasional excursions for comparatively brief periods across the Channel. They considered England much as the present English sovereigns do Ireland, namely, as a conquered country, which had become a possession and a dependency upon the crown, but not in any sense the seat of empire, and they utterly despised the native inhabitants. In view of these facts, the wonder that Richard, the King [Pg 176] of England, never spoke the English tongue at once disappears.

Preparing for war.

The conference broke up, and both sides prepared for war. Isaac, finding that he was not strong enough to resist such a horde of invaders as Richard brought with him, withdrew from his capital and retired to a fortress among the mountains. Richard then easily took possession of the town. A moderate force had been left to protect it; but Richard, promising his troops plenty of booty when they should get into it, led the way, waving his battle-axe in the air.

King Richard's battle-axe.

This battle-axe was a very famous weapon. It was one which Richard had caused to be made for himself before leaving England, and it was the wonder of the army on account of its size and weight. The object of a battle-axe was to break through the steel armor with which the knights and warriors of those days were accustomed to cover themselves, and which was proof against all ordinary blows. Now Richard was a man of prodigious personal strength, and, when fitting out his expedition in England, he caused an unusually large and heavy battle-axe to be made for himself, by way of showing his men what he could do in [Pg 177] swinging a heavy weapon. The head of this axe, or hammer, as perhaps it might more properly have been called, weighed twenty pounds, and most marvelous stories were told of the prodigious force of the blow that Richard could strike with it. When it came down on the head of a steel-clad knight on his horse, it broke through every thing, they said, and crushed man and horse both to the ground.

The conquest of Limesol.

The assault on Limesol was successful. The people made but a feeble resistance. Indeed, they had no weapons which could possibly enable them to stand a moment against the Crusaders. They were half naked, and their arms were little better than clubs and stones. They were, in consequence, very easily driven off the ground, and Richard took possession of the city.

Signaling for the queen's galley.

He then immediately made a signal for Joanna's galley—which, during all this time, had remained at the mouth of the harbor—to advance. The galley accordingly came up, and Joanna and the princess were received by the whole army at the landing with loud acclamations. They were immediately conducted into the town, and there were lodged splendidly in the best of Isaac's palaces.

[Pg 178]

But the contest was not yet ended. The place to which Isaac had retreated was a city which he possessed in the interior of the island called Nicosia. From this place he sent a messenger to Richard to propose another conference, with a view of attempting once more to agree upon some terms of peace. Richard agreed to this, and a place of meeting was appointed on a plain near Limesol, the port. King Isaac, accompanied by a suitable number of attendants, repaired to this place, and the conference was opened. Richard was mounted on a favorite Spanish charger, and was splendidly dressed in silk and gold. He assumed a very lofty bearing and demeanor toward his humbled enemy, and informed him in a very summary manner on what terms alone he was willing to make peace.

The terms of peace which Richard offered to Isaac.

"I will make peace with you," said Richard, "on condition that you hold your kingdom henceforth subject to me. You are to deliver up all the castles and strongholds to me, and do me homage as your acknowledged sovereign. You are also to pay me an ample indemnity in gold for the damage you did to my wrecked galleys. I shall expect you, moreover, to join me in the crusade. You must accompany me [Pg 179] to the Holy Land with not less than five hundred foot-soldiers, four hundred horsemen, and one hundred full-armed knights. For security that you will faithfully fulfill these conditions, you must put the princess, your daughter, into my hands as a hostage. Then, in case your conduct while in my service in the Holy

Land is in all respects perfectly satisfactory, I will restore your daughter, and also your castles, to you on my return."

Isaac's daughter was a very beautiful young princess. She was extremely beloved by her father, and was highly honored by the people of the land as the heir to the crown.

How Richard faithlessly took King Isaac a prisoner.

These conditions were certainly very hard, but the poor king was in no condition to resist any demands that Richard might choose to make. With much distress and anguish of mind, he pretended to agree to these terms, though he secretly resolved that he could not and would not submit to them. Richard suspected his sincerity, and, in utter violation of all honorable laws and usages of war, he made him a prisoner, and set guards over him to watch him until the stipulations should be carried into effect. Isaac contrived to escape from his keepers in the night, and, putting himself at [Pg 180] the head of such troops as he could obtain, prepared for war, with the determination to resist to the last extremity.

King Richard subjugates Cyprus.

Richard now resolved to proceed at once to take the necessary measures for the complete subjugation of the island. He organized a large body of land forces, and directed them to advance into the interior of the country, and put down all resistance. At the same time, he placed himself at the head of his fleet, and, sailing round the island, he took possession of all the towns and fortresses on the shore. He also seized every ship and every boat, large and small, that he could find, and thus entirely cut off from King Isaac all chance of escaping by sea. In the mean time, the unhappy monarch, with the few troops that still adhered to him, was driven from place to place, until at last he was completely hemmed in, and was compelled to fight or surrender. They fought. The result was what might have been expected. Richard was victorious. The capital, Limesol, fell into his hands, and the king and his daughter were taken prisoners.

The princess was greatly terrified when she was brought into Richard's presence. She fell on her knees before him, and cried,

[Pg 181]

"My lord the king, have mercy upon me!"

Richard put forth his hand to lift her up, and then sent her to Berengaria.

"I give her to you," said he, "for an attendant and companion."

The miserable death of King Isaac.

The king was almost broken-hearted at having his daughter taken away from him. He threw himself at Richard's feet, and begged him, with the most earnest entreaty, to restore him his child. Richard paid no heed to this request, but ordered Isaac to be taken away. Soon after this he sent him across the sea to Tripoli in Syria, and there shut him up in the dungeon of a castle, a hopeless prisoner. The unhappy captive was secured in his dungeon by chains; but, in honor of his rank, the chains, by Richard's directions, were made of silver, overlaid with gold. The poor king pined in this place of confinement for four years, and then died.

As soon as Isaac had gone, and things had become somewhat settled. Richard found himself undisputed master of Cyprus, and he resolved to annex the island to his own dominions.

"And now," said he to himself, "it will be a good time for me to be married."

Richard's wedding at last.

So, after making the necessary arrangements [Pg 182] for assembling his whole fleet again, and repairing the damages which had been sustained by the storm, he began to make preparations for the wedding. Berengaria made no objection to this. Indeed, the fright which she had suffered at sea in being separated from Richard, and the anxiety she had endured when, after the storm, she gazed in every direction all around the horizon, and could see no signs in any quarter of his ship, and when, consequently, she feared that he might be lost, made her extremely unwilling to be separated from him again.

A coronation.

The marriage was celebrated with great pomp and splendor, and many feasts and entertainments, and public parades, and celebrations followed, to commemorate the event. Among the other grand ceremonies was a coronation—a double coronation. Richard caused himself to be crowned King of Cyprus, and Berengaria Queen of England and of Cyprus too.

The king's accoutrement.

The dress in which Richard appeared on these occasions is minutely described. He wore a rose-colored satin tunic, which was fastened by a jeweled belt about his waist. Over this was a mantle of striped silver tissue, brocaded with silver half-moons. He wore an elegant and very costly sword too. The blade [Pg 183] was of Damascus steel, the hilt was of gold, and the scabbard was of silver, richly engraved in scales. On his head he wore a scarlet bonnet, brocaded in gold with figures of animals. He bore in his hand what was called a truncheon, which was a sort of sceptre, very splendidly covered and adorned.

Favelle.

He had an elegant horse—a Spanish charger—and wherever he went this horse was led before him, with the bits, and stirrups, and all the metallic mountings of the saddle and bridle in gold. The crupper was adorned with two golden lions, figured with their paws raised in the act of striking each other. Richard obtained another horse in Cyprus among the spoils that he acquired there, and which afterward became his favorite. His name was Favelle, though in some of the old annals he is called Faunelle. This horse acquired great fame by the strength and courage, and also the great sagacity, that he displayed in the various battles that he was engaged in with his master. Indeed, at last, he became quite a historical character.

Richard himself was a tall and well-formed man, and altogether a very fine-looking man, and in this costume, with his yellow curls and [Pg 184] bright complexion, he appeared, they said, a perfect model of military and manly grace.

The appearance of Berengaria.

There is a representation of Berengaria extant which is supposed to show her as she appeared at this time. Her hair is parted in the middle in front, and hangs down in long tresses behind. It is covered with a veil, open on each side, like a Spanish mantilla. The veil is fastened to her head by a royal diadem resplendent with gold and gems, and is surmounted with a *fleur de lis*, with so much foliage added to it as to give it the appearance of a double crown, in allusion to her being the queen both of Cyprus and of England.

The whole time occupied by these transactions in Cyprus was only about a month, and now, since every thing had been finished to his satisfaction, Richard began to think once more of prosecuting his voyage.

[Pg 185]

Chapter XI.

Voyage to Acre.

1190

The different names of Acre.

T he great landing-point for expeditions of Crusaders to the Holy Land was Acre, or Akka, as it is often written. The town was originally known as Ptolemais, and the situation of it may be found designated on ancient maps under that name. The Turks called it Akka, which name the French call Acre. It was also, after a certain time, called St. Jean d'Acre. It received this name from a famous military order that was founded in the Holy Land in the Middle Ages, called the Knights of St. John.

Order of St. John.

The origin of the order was as follows: About a hundred years before the time of Richard's crusade, a company of pious merchants from Naples, who went to Jerusalem, took pity, while they were there, on the pilgrims who came there to visit the Holy Sepulchre, and who, being poor, and very insufficiently provided for the journey, suffered a great many privations and hardships. These merchants accordingly built [Pg 186] and endowed a monastery, and made it the duty of the monks to receive and take care of a certain number of these pilgrims.

The Hospitalers.

They named the establishment the Monastery of St. John, and the monks themselves were called Hospitalers, their business being to receive and show hospitality to the pilgrims. So the monks were sometimes designated as the Hospitalers and sometimes the Brothers of St. John.

Knights of St. John.
Origin of the name of St. Jean d'Acre.

Other travelers, who came to Jerusalem from time to time, seeing this monastery, and observing the good which it was the means of effecting for the poor pilgrims, became interested in its welfare, and made grants and donations to it, by which, in the course of fifty years, it became much enlarged. At length, in process of time, a *military* order was connected with it. The pilgrims needed protection in going to and fro, as well as food, shelter, and rest at the end of their journey, and the military order was formed to furnish this protection. The knights of this order were called Knights Hospitalers, and sometimes Knights of St. John. The institution continued to grow, and finally the seat of it was transferred to Acre, which was a much more convenient place for giving succor to the [Pg 187] pilgrims, and also for fighting the Saracens, who were the great enemies that the pilgrims had to fear. From this time the institution was called St. John of Acre, as it was before St. John of Jerusalem, and finally its power and influence became so predominant in the town that the town itself was generally designated by the name of the institution, and it has been called St. Jean d'Acre to this day.

The order.

The order became at last very numerous. Great numbers of persons joined it from all the nations of Europe. They organized a regular government. They held fortresses and towns, and other territorial possessions of considerable value. They had a fleet, and an army, and a rich treasury. In a word, they became, as it were, a government and a nation.

The persons belonging to the order were divided into three classes:

1. *Knights.* — These were the armed men. They fought the battles, defended the pilgrims, managed the government, and performed all other similar functions.

2. *Chaplains.* — These were the priests and monks. They conducted worship, and attended, in general, to all the duties of devotion. They were the scholars, too, and acted as secretaries [Pg 188] and readers, whenever such duties were required.

3. *Servitors.* — The duty of the servitors was, as their name imports, to take charge of the buildings and grounds belonging to the order, to wait upon the sick, and accompany pilgrims, and to perform, in general, all other duties pertaining to their station.

[Pg 189-90]

THE RAMPARTS OF ACRE.
A description of the town of Acre.

The town of Acre stood on the shore of the sea, and was very strongly fortified. The walls and ramparts were very massive — altogether too thick and high to be demolished or scaled by any means of attack known in those days. The place had been in possession of the Knights of St. John, but in the course of the wars between the Saracens and the Crusaders that had prevailed before Richard came, it had fallen into the hands of the Saracens, and now the Crusaders were besieging it, in hopes to recover possession. They were encamped in thousands on a plain outside the town, in a beautiful situation overlooking the sea. Still farther back among the mountains were immense hordes of Saracens, watching an opportunity to come down upon the plain and overwhelm the Christian armies, while they, on the other hand, were making continued assaults upon the town, in [Pg 191] hopes of carrying it by storm, before their enemies on the mountains could attack them. Of course, the Crusaders were extremely anxious to have Richard arrive, for they knew that he was bringing with him an immense re-enforcement.

Philip before Acre.
The siege.

Philip, the French king, had already arrived, and he exerted himself to the utmost to take the town before Richard should come. But he could not succeed. The town resisted all the attempts he could make to storm it, and, in the mean time, his position and that of the other Crusaders in the camp was becoming very critical, on account of the immense numbers of Saracens in the mountains behind them, who were gradually advancing their posts and threatening to surround the Christians entirely. Philip, therefore, and the forces joined with him, were beginning to feel very anxious to see Richard's ships drawing near, and from their encampment on the plain they looked out over the sea, and watched day after day, earnestly in hopes that they might see the advanced ships of Richard's fleet coming into view in the offing.

In the mean time, Richard, having sailed from Cyprus, was coming on, though he was delayed on his way by an occurrence which he greatly [Pg 192] gloried in, deeming it doubtless a very brilliant exploit. The case was this:

Chasing a Saracen vessel.

In sailing along with his squadron between Cyprus and the main land, he suddenly fell in with a ship of very large size. At first Richard and his men wondered what ship it could be. It was soon evident that, whatever she was, she was endeavoring to escape. Richard ordered his galleys to press on, and he soon found that the strange ship was full of Saracens. He immediately ordered his men to advance and board her, and he declared to his seamen that if they allowed her to escape he would crucify them.

Desperation.

The Saracens, seeing that there was no possibility of escape, and having no hope of mercy if they fell into Richard's hands, determined to scuttle the ship, and to sink themselves and the vessel together. They accordingly cut holes through the bottom as well as they could with hatchets, and the water began to pour in. In the mean time, Richard's galleys had surrounded the vessel, and a dreadful combat ensued. Both parties fought like tigers. The Crusaders were furious to get on board before the ship should go down, and the Saracens, though they had no expectation of finally defending themselves [Pg 193] against their enemies, still hoped to keep them back until it should be too late for them to obtain any advantage from their victory.

The terrible Greek fire which the Saracens used.

For a time they were quite successful in their resistance, chiefly by means of what was called Greek fire. This Greek fire was a celebrated means of warfare in those days, and was very terrible in its nature and effects. It is not known precisely what it was, or how it was made. It was an exceedingly combustible substance, and was to be thrown, on fire, at the enemy; and such was its nature, that when once in flames nothing could extinguish it; and, besides the heat and burning that it produced, it threw out great volumes of poisonous and stifling vapors, which suffocated all that came near. The men threw it sometimes in balls, sometimes on the ends of darts and arrows, where it was enveloped in flax or tow to keep it in its place. It burned fiercely and furiously wherever it fell. Even water did not extinguish it, and it was said that in this combat the sea all around the Saracens' ship seemed on fire, and the decks of the galleys that attacked them were blazing with it in every direction. Great numbers of Richard's men were killed by it.

The ship is taken.
A massacre.

But the superiority of numbers on Richard's [Pg 194] side was too great, and after a time the Saracens were subdued, before the ship had admitted water enough through the scuttlings to carry her down. Richard's men poured in on board of her in great numbers. They immediately proceeded to massacre or throw overboard the men as fast as possible, and to seize the stores and transfer them to their own ships. They also did all they could to stop the leaks, so as to delay the sinking of the ship as long as possible. They had time to transfer to their own vessels nearly all the valuable part of the cargo, and to kill and drown all the men. Out of twelve or fifteen hundred, only about thirty-five were spared.

Richard's defense.
King Richard's cupidity.

When, afterward, public sentiment seemed inclined to condemn this terrible and inexcusable massacre, Richard defended himself by saying that he found on board the vessel a number of jars containing certain poisonous reptiles, which he alleged the Saracens were going to take to Acre, and there let them loose near the Crusaders' camp to bite the soldiers, and that men who could resort to so barbarous a mode of warfare as this deserved no quarter. However this may be, the poor Saracens received no quarter. It might be supposed that Richard [Pg 195] deserved some credit for his humanity in saving the thirty-five. But his object in saving these was not to show mercy, but to gain ransom-money. These thirty-five were the *emirs*, or other officers of the Saracens, or persons who looked as if they might be rich or have rich friends. When they reached the shore, Richard fixed upon a certain sum of money for each of them, and allowed them to send word to their friends that if they would raise that money and send it to Richard, he would set them at liberty. A great proportion of them were thus afterward ransomed, and Richard realized from this source quite a large sum.

The sinking ship.

When Richard's soldiers found that the time for the captured ship to sink was drawing nigh, they abandoned her, leaving on board every thing that they had not been able to save, and, withdrawing to a safe distance, they saw her go down. The sea all around her was covered with the bodies of the dead and dying, and also with bales of merchandise, broken weapons, fragments of the wreck, and with the flickering and exhausted remnants of the Greek fire.

The fleet then got under way again, and pursued its course to Acre.

[Pg 196]

Chapter XII.

The Arrival at Acre.

1190
The besieging army at Acre.

While Richard was thus, with his fleet, drawing near to Acre, the armies of the Crusaders that were besieging the town had been for some time gradually getting into a very critical situation. This army was made up of a great many different bodies of troops, that had come in the course of years from all parts of Europe to recover the Holy Land from the possession of the unbelievers. There were Germans, and French, and Normans, and Italians, and people from the different kingdoms of Spain, with knights, and barons, and earls, and bishops, and archbishops, and princes, and other dignitaries of all kinds without number. With such a heterogeneous mass there could be no common bond, nor any general and central authority. They spoke a great variety of languages, and were accustomed to very different modes of warfare; and the several orders of knights, and the different bodies of troops, were continually getting involved in dissensions arising [Pg 197] from the jealousies and rivalries which they bore to each other. The enemy, on the other hand, were united under the command of one great and powerful Saracen leader named Saladin.

Motives of the Saracens.
Motives of the Christians.

There was another great difference between the Crusaders and the Saracens which was greatly to the advantage of the latter. The Saracens were fighting simply to deliver their country from these bands of invaders. Thus their object was *one*. If any part of the army achieved a success, the other divisions rejoiced at it, for it tended to advance them all toward the common end that all had in view. On the other hand, the chief end and aim of the Crusaders was to get glory to themselves in the estimation of friends and neighbors at home, and of Europe in general. It is true that they desired to obtain this glory by victories over the unbelievers and the conquest of the Holy Land, but these last objects were the means and not the end. The *end*, in their view, was their own personal glory. The consequence was, that while the Saracens would naturally all rejoice at an advantage gained over the enemy by any portion of their army, yet in the camp of the Crusaders, if one body of knights performed [Pg 198] a great deed of strength or bravery which was likely to attract attention in Europe, the rest were apt to be disappointed and vexed instead of being pleased. They were envious of the fame which the successful party had acquired. In a word, when an advantage was gained by any particular body of troops, the rest did not think of the benefit to the common cause which had thereby been secured, but only of the danger that the fame acquired by those who gained it might eclipse or outshine their own renown.

Envyings and jealousy among the besiegers.
King of Jerusalem.

The various orders of knights and the commanders of the different bodies of troops vied with each other, not only in respect to the acquisition of glory, but also in the elegance of their arms, the splendor of their tents and banners, the beauty and gorgeous caparisons of the horses, and the pomp and parade with which they conducted all their movements and operations. The camp was full of quarrels, too, among the great leaders in respect to the command of the places in the Holy Land which had been conquered in previous campaigns. These places, as fast as they had been taken, had been made principalities and kingdoms, to give titles of rank to the crusaders who had taken them; [Pg 199] and, though the places themselves had in many instances been lost again, and given up to the Saracens, the titles remained to be quarreled about among the Crusaders. There was particularly a great quarrel at this time about the title of King of Jerusalem. It was a mere empty title, for Jerusalem was in the hands of the Saracens, but there were twenty very powerful and influential claimants to it, each of whom manœuvred and intrigued incessantly with all the other knights and commanders in the army to gain partisans to his side. Thus the camp of the Crusaders, from one cause and another, had become one universal scene of rivalry, jealousy, and discord.

A common danger makes a common cause.

There was a small approach toward a greater degree of unity of feeling just before the time of Richard's arrival, produced by the common danger to which they began to see they were exposed. They had been now two years besieging Acre, and had accomplished nothing. All the furious attempts that they had made to storm the place had been unsuccessful. The walls were too thick and solid for the battering-rams to make any serious impression upon them, and the garrison within were so numerous and so well armed, and they hurled down [Pg 200] such a tremendous shower of darts, javelins, stones, and other missiles of every kind upon all who came near, that immense numbers of those who were brought up near the walls to work the engines were killed, while the besieged themselves, being protected by the battlements on the walls, were comparatively safe.

The terrible loss of life in the siege of Acre.
The unwieldy armor of the knights.

In the course of the two years during which the siege had now been going on, bodies of troops from all parts of Europe had been continually coming and going, and as in those days there was far less of system and organization in the conduct of military affairs than there is now, the camp was constantly kept in a greater or less degree of confusion, so that it is impossible to know with certainty how many were engaged, and what the actual loss of life had been. The lowest estimate is that one hundred and fifty thousand men perished before Acre during this siege, and some historians calculate the loss at five hundred thousand. The number of deaths was greatly increased by the plague, which prevailed at one time among the troops, and committed fearful ravages. One thing, however, must be said, in justice to the reckless and violent men who commanded these bands, and that is, that they did not send their poor, [Pg 201] helpless followers, the common soldiers, into a danger which they kept out of themselves. It was a point of honor with them to take the foremost rank, and to expose themselves fully at all times to the worst dangers of the combat. It is true that the knights and nobles were better protected by their armor than the soldiers. They were generally covered with steel from head to foot, and so heavily loaded with it were they, that it was only on horseback that they could sustain themselves in battle at all. Indeed, it was said that if a full-armed knight, in those days, were, from any accident, unhorsed, his armor was so heavy that, if he were thrown down upon the ground in his fall, he could not possibly get up again without help.

Notwithstanding this protection, however, the knights and commanders exposed themselves so much that they suffered in full proportion with the rest. It was estimated that during the siege there fell in battle, or perished of sickness or fatigue, eighteen or twenty archbishops and bishops, forty earls, and no less than five hundred barons, all of whose names are recorded. So they obtained what they went for—commemoration in history. Whether the reward was worth the price they paid for it, in sacrificing [Pg 202] every thing like happiness and usefulness in life, and throwing themselves, after a few short months of furious and angry warfare, into a bloody grave, is a very serious question.

King Richard received by the besieging army.

As soon as Richard's fleet appeared in view, the whole camp was thrown into a state of the wildest commotion. The drums were beat, the trumpets were sounded, and flags and banners without number were waved in the air. The troops were paraded, and when the ships arrived at the shore, and Richard and his immediate attendants and followers landed, they were received by the commanders of the Crusaders' army on the beach with the highest honors, while the soldiers drawn up around filled the air with long and loud acclamations.

Berengaria a bride.

Berengaria had come from Cyprus, not in Richard's ship, although she was now married to him. She had continued in her own galley, and was still under the charge of her former guardian, Stephen of Turnham. That ship had been fitted up purposely for the use of the queen and the princess, and the arrangements on board were more suitable for the accommodation of ladies than were those of Richard's ship, which being strictly a war vessel, and intended always [Pg 203] to be foremost in every fight, was arranged solely with a view to the purposes of battle, and was therefore not a very suitable place for a bride.

Philip's conciliation.

Berengaria and Joanna landed very soon after Richard. Philip was a little piqued at the suddenness with which Richard had married another lady, so soon after the engagement with Alice had been terminated; but he considered how urgent the necessity was that he should now be on good terms with his ally, and so he concealed his feelings, and received Berengaria himself as she came from her ship, and assisted her to land.

[Pg 204]

Chapter XIII.

Difficulties.

1191

I t was but a very short time after Richard had landed his forces at Acre, and had taken his position in the camp on the plain before the city, before serious difficulties began to arise between him and Philip. This, indeed, might have been easily foreseen. It was perfectly certain that, so soon as Richard should enter the camp of the Crusaders, he would immediately assume such airs of superiority, and attempt to lord it over all the other kings and princes there in so reckless and dictatorial a manner, that there could be no peace with him except in entire submission to his will.

Richard's arrogance produces dissension in the camp.

This was, accordingly, soon found to be the case. He began to quarrel with Philip in a very short time, notwithstanding the sincere desire that Philip manifested to live on good terms with him. Of course, the knights and barons, and, after a time, the common soldiers in the two armies, took sides with their respective sovereigns. One great source of trouble was, that Richard claimed to be the feudal sovereign [Pg 205] of Philip himself, on account of some old claims that he advanced, as Duke of Normandy, over the French kingdom. This pretension Philip, of course, would not admit, and the question gave rise to endless disputes and heartburnings.

The progress of the quarrel between Richard and Philip.

Presently the quarrel extended to other portions of the army of the Crusaders, and the different orders of knights and bodies of soldiers espoused, some one side and some the other. The Knights Hospitalers, described in a former chapter, who had now become a numerous and very powerful force, took Richard's side. Indeed, Richard was personally popular among the knights and barons generally, on account of his prodigious strength and the many feats of reckless daring that he performed. When he went out every body flocked to see him, and the whole camp was full of the stories that were told of his wonderful exploits. He made use of the distinction which he thus acquired as a means of overshadowing Philip's influence and position. This Philip, of course, resented, and then the English said that he was envious of Richard's superiority; and they attempted to lay the whole blame of the quarrel on him, attributing the unfriendly feeling simply to what they considered his weak and ungenerous [Pg 206] jealousy of a more successful and fortunate rival.

However this may be, the disagreement soon became so great that the two kings could no longer co-operate together in fighting against their common enemy.

The English and French armies no longer co-operate.

Philip planned an assault against the town. He was going to take it by storm. Richard did not join him in this attempt. He made it an excuse that he was sick at the time. Indeed, he was sick not long after his arrival at Acre, but whether his illness really prevented his co-operating with Philip in the assault, or was only made use of as a pretext, is not quite certain. At any rate, Richard left Philip to make the assault alone, and the consequence was that the French troops were driven back from the walls with great loss. Richard secretly rejoiced at this discomfiture, but Philip was in a great rage.

Not long afterward Richard planned an assault, to be executed with *his* troops alone; for Philip now stood aloof, and refused to aid him. Richard had no objection to this; indeed, he rejoiced in an opportunity to show the world that he could succeed in accomplishing a feat of arms after Philip had attempted it and failed.

[Pg 207-8]

THE ASSAULT.

[Pg 209]

Preparations for an assault.

So he brought forward the engines that he had caused to be built at Messina, and set them up. He organized his assaulting columns and prepared for the attack. He made the scaling-ladders ready, and provided his men with great stores of ammunition; and when the appointed day at length arrived, he led his men on to the assault, fully confident that he was about to perform an exploit that would fill all Europe with his fame.

A repulse.

But, unfortunately for him, he was doomed to disappointment. His men were driven back from the walls. The engines were over-thrown and broken to pieces, or set on fire by flaming javelins sent from the walls, and burned to the ground. Vast numbers of his soldiers were killed, and at length, all hope of success having disappeared, the troops were drawn off, discomfited and excessively chagrined.

Reflections.
Dangers of the army.

The reflections which would naturally follow in the minds of Philip and Richard, as they sat in their tents moodily pondering on

129

these failures, led them to think that it would be better for them to cease quarreling with each other, and to combine their strength against the common enemy. Indeed, their situation was now fast becoming very critical, inasmuch as every [Pg 210] day during which the capture of the town was delayed the troops of Saladin on the mountains around them were gradually increasing in numbers, and gaining in the strength of their position, and they might at any time now be expected to come pouring down upon the plain in such force as entirely to overwhelm the whole army of the Crusaders.

A nominal friendship between real enemies.

So Richard and Philip made an agreement with each other that they would thenceforth live together on better terms, and endeavor to combine their strength against the common enemy, instead of wasting it in petty quarrels with each other.

From this time things went on much better in the camp of the allies, while yet there was no real or cordial friendship between Richard and Philip, or any of their respective partisans. Richard attempted secretly to entice away knights and soldiers from Philip's service by offering them more money or better rewards than Philip paid them, and Philip, when he discovered this, attempted to retaliate by endeavoring to buy off, in the same manner, some of Richard's men. In a word, the fires of the feud, though covered up and hidden, were burning away underneath as fiercely as ever.

[Pg 211]

Chapter XIV.

The Fall of Acre.

1191

The distress of the besieged city.
Famine.
Disappointed hopes.

Although the allies failed to reduce Acre by assault, the town was at last compelled to submit to them through the distress and misery to which the inhabitants and the garrison were finally reduced by famine. They bore these sufferings as long as they could, but the time arrived at last when they could be endured no longer. They hoped for some relief which was to have been sent to them by sea from Cairo, but it did not come. They also hoped, day after day, and week after week, that Saladin would be strong enough to come down from the mountains, and break through the camp of the Crusaders on the plain and rescue them. But they were disappointed. The Crusaders had fortified their camp in the strongest manner, and then they were so numerous and so fully armed that Saladin thought it useless to make any general attack upon them with the force that he had under his command.

The various methods of warfare.
Undermining the walls.
The effect on the walls.

The siege had continued two years when [Pg 212] Philip and Richard arrived. They came early in the spring of 1191. Of course, their arrival greatly strengthened the camp of the besiegers, and went far to extinguish the remaining hopes of the garrison. The commanders, however, did not immediately give up, but held out some months longer, hoping every day for the arrival of the promised relief from Cairo. In the mean time, they continued to endure a succession of the most vigorous assaults from the Crusaders, of which very marvelous tales are told in the romantic narratives of those times. In these narratives we have accounts of the engines which Richard set up opposite the walls, and of the efforts made by the besieged to set them on fire; of Richard's working, himself, like any common soldier in putting these engines together, and in extinguishing the flames when they were set on fire; of a vast fire-proof shed which was at last contrived to cover and protect the engines — the covering of the roof being made fire-proof with green hides; and of a plan which was finally adopted, when it was found that the walls could not be beaten down by battering-rams, of undermining them with a view of making them tumble down by their own weight. In this case, the workmen who undermined the [Pg 213] walls were protected at their work by sheds built over them, and, in order to prevent the walls from falling upon them while they were mining, they propped them up with great beams of wood, so placed that they could make fires under the beams when they were ready for the walls to fall, and then have time to retreat to a safe distance before they should be burned through. This plan, however, did not succeed; for the walls were so prodigiously thick, and the blocks of stone of which they were composed were so firmly bound together, that, instead of falling into a mass of ruins, as Richard had expected, when the props had been burned through, they only settled down bodily on one side into the excavation, and remained nearly as good, for all purposes of defense, as ever.

A spy in the city.
The letters which came on arrows.

It was said that during the siege Richard and Philip obtained a great deal of information in respect to the plans of the Saracens through the instrumentality of some secret friend within the city, who contrived to find means of continually sending them important intelligence. This intelligence related sometimes to the designs of the garrison in respect to sorties that they were going to make, or to the secret plans that they had formed for procuring supplies of [Pg 214] provisions or other succor; at other times they related to the movements and designs of Saladin, who was outside among the mountains, and especially to the attacks that he was contemplating on the allied camp. This intelligence was communicated in various ways. The principal method was to send a letter by means of an arrow. An arrow frequently came down in some part of the allied camp, which, on being examined, was found to have a letter wound about the shaft. The letter was addressed to Richard, and was, of course, immediately carried to his tent. It was always found to contain very important information in respect to the condition or plans of the besieged. If a sortie was intended from the city, it stated the time and the place, and detailed all the arrangements, thus enabling Richard to be on his guard. So, if the Saracens were projecting an attack on the lines from within, the whole plan of it was fully explained, and, of course, it would then be very easy for Richard to frustrate it. The writer of the letters said that he was a Christian, but would not say who he was, and the mystery was never explained. It is quite possible that there is very little truth in the whole story.

[Pg 215]

A flag of truce.

At all events, though the assaults which the allies made against the walls and bulwarks of the town were none of them wholly successful, the general progress of the siege was altogether in their favor, and against the poor Saracens shut up within it. The last hope which they indulged was that some supplies would come to them by sea; but Richard's fleet, which remained at anchor off the town, blockaded the port so completely that there was no possibility that any thing could get in. The last lingering hope was, therefore, at length abandoned, and when the besieged found that they could endure their horrible misery no longer, they sent a flag of truce out to the camp of the besiegers, with a proposal to negotiate terms of surrender.

Terms proposed by the Saracens.
Richard's exactions and his threats.

Then followed a long negotiation, with displays of haughty arrogance on one side, and heart-broken and bitter humiliation on the other. The Saracens first proposed what they considered fair and honorable terms, and Philip was disposed to accept them; but Richard rejected them with scorn. After a vain attempt at resistance, Philip was obliged to yield, and to allow his imperious and overbearing ally to have his own way. The Saracens wished to stipulate for the lives of the garrison, but Richard [Pg 216] refused. He told them they must submit unconditionally; and, for his part, he did not care, he said, whether they yielded now or continued the contest. He should soon be in possession of the city, at any rate, and if they held out until he took it by storm, then, of course, it would be given up to the unbridled fury of the soldiers, who would mercilessly massacre every living thing they should find in it, and seize every species of property as plunder. This, he declared, was sure to be the end of the siege, and that very soon, unless they chose to submit. The Saracens then asked what terms he required of them. Richard stated his terms, and they asked for a little time to consider them and to confer with Saladin, who, being the sultan, was their sovereign, and without his approval they could not act.

The convention.
Hostages.
The ransom of the captives.

So the negotiation was opened, and, after various difficulties and delays, a convention was finally agreed upon. The terms were these:

I. The city was to be surrendered to the allied armies, and all the arms, ammunition, military stores, and property of all kinds which it contained were to be forfeited to the conquerors.

[Pg 217]

II. The troops and the people of the town were to be allowed to go free on the payment of a ransom.

III. The ransom by which the besieged purchased their lives and liberty was to be made up as follows:

1. The wood of the cross on which Christ was crucified, which was alleged to be in Saladin's possession, was to be restored.

2. Saladin was to set at liberty the Christian captives which he had taken in the course of the war from various armies of Crusaders, and which he now held as prisoners. The number of these prisoners was about fifteen hundred.

3. He was to pay two hundred thousand pieces of gold.

IV. Richard was to retain a large body of men—it was said that there were about five thousand in all—consisting of soldiers of the garrison or inhabitants of the town, as hostages for the fulfillment of these conditions. These men were to be kept forty days, or, if at the end of that time Saladin had not fulfilled the conditions of the surrender, they were all to be put to death.

[Pg 218]

Saladin's assent.

Perhaps Saladin agreed to these terms, under the pressure of dire necessity, compelled as he was to assent to whatever Richard might propose by the dreadful extremity to which the town was reduced, without sufficiently considering whether he would be really able to fulfill his promises. At any rate, these were the promises that he made; and as soon as the treaty was duly executed, the gates of Acre were opened to the conquerors, while Saladin himself broke up his encampment on the mountains, and withdrew his troops farther into the interior of the country.

Richard enters Acre in triumph.
The Archduke of Austria's banner.

Although the treaty was made and executed in the name of both the kings, Richard had taken into his hands almost the whole conduct of the negotiation, and now that the army was about to take possession of the town, he considered himself the conqueror of it. He entered with great parade, assigning to Philip altogether a secondary part in the ceremony. He also took possession of the principal palace of the place as his quarters, and there established himself with Berengaria and Joanna, while he left Philip to take up his residence wherever he could. The flags of both monarchs were, however, raised upon the walls, and so far Philip's [Pg 219] claim to a joint sovereignty over the place was acknowledged. But none of the other princes or potentates who had been engaged in the siege were allowed to share this honor. One of them—the Archduke of Austria—ventured to raise his banner on one of the towers, but Richard pulled it down, tore it to pieces, and trampled it under his feet.

This, of course, threw the archduke into a dreadful rage, and most of the other smaller princes in the army shared the indignation that he felt at the grasping disposition which Richard manifested, and at his violent and domineering behavior. But they were helpless. Richard was stronger than they, and they were compelled to submit.

Philip in trouble.
Philip's secret plans.

As for Philip, he had long since begun to find his situation extremely disagreeable. He was very sensitive to the overbearing and arrogant treatment which he received, but he either had not the force of character or the physical strength to resist it. Now, since Acre had fallen, he found his situation worse than ever. There was no longer any enemy directly before them, and it was only the immediate presence of an enemy that had thus far kept Richard within any sort of bounds. Philip saw now [Pg 220] plainly that if he were to remain in the Holy Land, and attempt to continue the war, he could only do it by occupying an altogether secondary and subordinate position, and to this he thought it was wholly inconsistent with his rights and dignities as an independent sovereign to descend; so he began to revolve secretly in his mind how he could honorably withdraw from the expedition and return home.

Title of King of Jerusalem.
Sibylla.

While things were in this state, a great quarrel, which had for a long time been gradually growing up in the camp of the Crusaders, but had been restrained and kept, in some degree, subdued by the excitement of the siege, broke out in great violence. The question was who should claim the title of King of Jerusalem. Jerusalem was at this time in the hands of the Saracens, so that the title was, for the time being at least, a mere empty name. Still, there was a very fierce contention to decide who should possess it. It seems that it had originally descended to a certain lady named Sibylla. It had come down to her as the descendant and heir of a very celebrated crusader named Godfrey of Bouillon, who was the first king of Jerusalem. He became King of Jerusalem by having headed the army of Crusaders that first [Pg 221] conquered it from the Saracens. This was about a hundred years before the time of the taking of Acre. The knights and generals of his army elected him King of Jerusalem a short time after he had taken it, and the title descended from him to Sibylla.

Guy of Lusignan.
Isabella.
Conrad of Montferrat.

Sibylla was married to a famous knight named Guy of Lusignan, and he claimed the title of King of Jerusalem in right of his wife. This claim was acknowledged by the rest of the Crusaders so long as Sibylla lived, but at length she died, and then many persons maintained that the crown descended to her sister Isabella. Isabella was married to a knight named Humphrey of Huron, who had not strength or resolution enough to assert his claims. Indeed, he had the reputation of being a weak and timid man. Accordingly, another knight, named Conrad of Montferrat, conceived the idea of taking his place. He contrived to seize and bear away the Lady Isabella, and afterward to procure a divorce for her from her husband, and then, finally, he married her himself. He now claimed to be King of Jerusalem in right of Isabella, while Guy of Lusignan maintained that his right to the crown still continued. This was a nice question to be settled by such a rude horde of [Pg 222] fighting men as these Crusaders were, and some took one side of it and some the other, according as their various ideas on the subject of rights of succession or their personal partialities inclined them.

The positions of Richard and Philip respecting the title.

Now it happened that Philip and Richard had early taken opposite sides in respect to this affair, as indeed they did on almost every other subject that came before them. Guy of Lusignan had gone to visit Richard while he was in Cyprus, and there, having had the field all to himself, had told his story in such a way, and also made such proposals and promises, as to enlist Richard in his favor. Richard there agreed that he would take Guy's part in the controversy, and he furnished him with a sum of money at that time to relieve his immediate necessities. He did this with a view of securing Guy, as one of his partisans and adherents, in any future difficulties in which he might be involved in the course of the campaign.

One of Richard's compromises.

On the other hand, when Philip arrived at Acre, which it will be recollected was some time before Richard came, the friends and partisans of Conrad, who were there, at once proceeded to lay Conrad's case before him, and they so far succeeded as to lead Philip to commit himself [Pg 223] on that side. Thus the foundation of a quarrel on this subject was laid before Richard landed. The quarrel was kept down, however, during the progress of the siege, but when at length the town was taken it broke out anew, and the whole body of the Crusaders became greatly agitated with it. At length some sort of compromise was effected, or at least what was called a compromise, but really, so far as the substantial interests involved were concerned, Richard had it all his own way. This affair still further alienated Philip's mind from his ally, and made him more desirous than ever to abandon the enterprise and return home.

Philip announces his return.

Accordingly, after the two kings had been established in Acre a short time, Philip announced that he was sick, and unable any longer to prosecute the war in person, and that he was intending to return home. When this was announced to Richard, he exclaimed,

"Shame on him! eternal shame! and on all his kingdom, if he goes off and abandons us now before the work is done."

Richard's objections to Philip's return.

The work which Richard meant to have done was the complete recovery of the Holy Land from the possession of the Saracens. The taking of Acre was a great step, but, after all, it was [Pg 224] only a beginning. The army of the allies was now to march into the interior of the country to pursue Saladin, in hopes of conquering him in a general battle, and so at length gaining possession of the whole country and recovering Jerusalem. Richard, therefore, was very indignant with Philip for being disposed to abandon the enterprise while the work to be accomplished was only just begun.

There was another reason why Richard was alarmed at the idea of Philip's returning home.

"He will take advantage of my absence," said he, "and invade my dominions, and so, when I return, I shall find that I have been robbed of half my provinces."

So Richard did all he could to dissuade Philip from returning; but at length, finding that he could produce no impression on his mind, he yielded, and gave a sort of surly consent to the arrangement. "Let him go," said he, "if he will. Poor man! He is sick, he says, and I suppose he thinks he can not live unless he can see Paris again."

Richard insisted, however, that if Philip went he should leave his army behind, or, at least, a large portion of it; so Philip agreed to leave ten thousand men. These men were to be under [Pg 225] the command of the Duke of Burgundy, one of Philip's most distinguished nobles. The duke, however, himself was to be subject to the orders of Richard.

Philip's oath to Richard.

Richard also exacted of Philip a solemn oath, that when he had returned to France he would not, in any way, molest or invade any of his—that is, Richard's—possessions, or make war against any of his vassals or allies. This agreement was to continue in force, and to be binding upon Philip until forty days after Richard should have himself returned from the Crusade.

Disapprobation of King Philip's course.

These things being all thus arranged, Philip began to make his preparations openly for embarking on his voyage home. The knights and barons, and indeed the whole body of the army, considered Philip's leaving them as a very culpable abandonment of the enterprise, and they crowded around the place of embarkation when he went on board his vessel, and manifested their displeasure with ill-suppressed hisses and groans.

Saladin is unable to fulfill his promises.

The time which had been fixed upon for Saladin to comply with the stipulations of the surrender was forty days, and this period was now, after Philip had gone, drawing rapidly to a close. [Pg 226] Saladin found that he could not fulfill the conditions to which he had agreed. As the day approached he made various excuses and apologies to Richard, and he also sent him a number of costly presents, hoping, perhaps, in that way to propitiate his favor, and prevent his insisting on the execution of the dreadful penalty which had been agreed upon in case of default, namely, the slaughter of the five thousand hostages which had been left in his hands.

Brutality of Richard.

The time at last expired, and the treaty had not been fulfilled. Richard, without waiting even a day, determined that the hostages should be slain. A rumor was set in circulation that Saladin had put to death all his Christian prisoners. This rumor was false, but it served its purpose of exasperating the minds of the Crusaders, so as to bring the soldiers up well to the necessary pitch of ferocity for executing so terrible a work. The slaughter of five thousand defenseless and unresisting men, in cold blood, is a very hard work for even soldiers to perform, and if such a work is to be done, it is always necessary to contrive some means of heating the blood of the executioners in order to insure the accomplishment of it. In this case, the rumor that Saladin had murdered his Christian [Pg 227] prisoners was more than sufficient. It wrought up the allied army to such a phrensy that the soldiers assembled in crowds, and riotously demanded that the Saracen prisoners should be given up to them, in order that they might have their revenge.

The massacre of the Saracen captives.

Accordingly, at the appointed time, Richard gave the command, and the whole body of the prisoners were brought out, and conducted to the plain beyond the lines of the encampment. A few were reserved. These were persons of rank and consideration, who were to be saved in hopes that they might have wealthy friends at home who would pay money to ransom them. The rest were divided into two portions, one of which was committed to the charge of the Duke of Burgundy, and the other Richard led himself. The dreadful processions formed by these wretched men were followed by the excited soldiery that were to act as their executioners, who came crowding on in throngs, waving their swords, and filling the air with their ferocious threats and imprecations, and exulting in the prospect of having absolutely their fill of the pleasure of killing men, without any danger to themselves to mar the enjoyment of it.

The massacre was carried into effect in the [Pg 228] fullest possible manner; and after the men were killed, the Christians occupied themselves in cutting open their bodies to find jewels and other articles of value, which they pretended that the poor captives had swallowed in order to hide them from their enemies.

Richard's exultation.
Supernatural approval.

Instead of being ashamed of this deed, Richard gloried in it. He considered it a wonderful proof of his zeal for the cause of Christ. The writers of the time praised it. The Saracens, they maintained, were the enemies of God, and whoever slew them did God service. One of the historians of the time says that angels from heaven appeared to Richard at the time, and urged him to persevere to the end, crying aloud to him while the massacre was going on, "Kill! kill! Spare them not!"

It seems to us at the present day most amazing that the minds of men could possibly be so perverted as to think that in performing such deeds as this they were sustaining the cause of the meek and gentle Jesus of Nazareth, and were the objects of approval and favor with God, the common father of us all, who has declared that he has made of one blood all the nations of the earth, to live together in peace and unity.

[Pg 229]

Chapter XV.

Progress of the Crusade.

1191

Richard leaving Acre.
Modern warfare.

T he first thing which Richard had now to do, before commencing a march into the interior of the country, was to set every thing in order at Acre, and to put the place in a good condition of defense, in case it should be attacked while he was gone. The walls in many places were to be repaired, particularly where they had been undermined by Richard's sappers, and in many places, too, they had been broken down or greatly damaged by the action of the battering-rams and other engines. In the case of sieges prosecuted by means of artillery in modern times, the whole interior of the town, as well as the walls, is usually battered dreadfully by the shot and shells that are thrown over into it. A shell, which is a hollow ball of iron sometimes more than a foot in diameter, and with sides two or three inches thick, and filled within with gunpowder, is thrown from a mortar, at a distance of some miles, high into the air over the town, whence [Pg 230] it descends into the streets or among the houses. The engraving represents the form of the mortar, and the manner in which the shell is thrown from it, though in this case the shell represented is directed, not against the town, but is thrown from a battery under the walls of the town against the camp or the trenches of the besiegers.

[Pg 231-2]

THROWING SHELLS.
Contrast between modern and ancient weapons.

These shells, of course, when they descend, come crashing through the roofs of the buildings on which they strike, or bury themselves in the ground if they fall in the street, and then burst with a terrific explosion. A town that has been bombarded in a siege becomes sometimes almost a mere mass of ruins. Often the bursting of a shell sets a building on fire, and then the dreadful effects of a conflagration are added to the horrors of the scene. In ancient sieges, on the other hand, none of these terrible agencies could be employed. The battering-rams could touch nothing but the walls and the outer towers, and it was comparatively very little injury that they could do to these. The javelins and arrows, and other light missiles—even those that were thrown from the military engines, if by chance they passed over the walls and entered the town, could do no serious mischief to the buildings there. The worst that [Pg 233] could happen from them was the wounding or killing of some person in the streets who might, just at that moment, be passing by.

Purifying the places of pagan worship.

In repairing Acre, therefore, and putting it again in a perfect condition for defense, nothing but the outer walls required attention.

Richard set companies of workmen upon these, and before long every thing was restored as it was before. There were then some ceremonies to be performed within the town, to purify it from the pollution which it had sustained by having been in the possession of the Saracens. All the Christian churches particularly, and the monasteries and other religious houses, were to be thus restored from the desecration which they had undergone, and consecrated anew to the service of Christ.

Revelings of the soldiery.

In the mean time, while these works and performances were going on, the soldiers gave themselves up to indulgences of every kind. Great stores of wine were found in the place, which were bestowed upon the troops, and the streets, day and night, were filled with riotous revelings. The commanders themselves—the knights and barons—and all the other men of rank that pertained to the army, fell into the same way, and they were very unwilling that the time should [Pg 234] come when they were to leave such a place of security and indulgence, and take the field again for a march in pursuit of Saladin.

The object of the Crusades was the recovery of the Holy Sepulchre.

At length, however, the time arrived when the march must be commenced. Richard had learned, by means of scouts and spies which he sent out, that Saladin was moving to the southward and westward—retreating, in fact, toward Jerusalem, which was, of course, the great point that he wished to defend. That, indeed, was the great point of attack, for the main object which the Crusaders proposed to themselves in invading Palestine was to get possession of the sepulchre where Christ was buried at Jerusalem. The recovery of the Holy Sepulchre was the watchword; and among all the people who were watching the progress of the enterprise with so much solicitude, and also among the Crusaders themselves, the progress that was made was valued just in proportion as it tended to the accomplishment of this end.

Order of the march from Acre.

Richard set apart a sufficient number of troops for a garrison to hold and defend Acre, and then, on taking a census of the remainder of his force, found that he had thirty thousand men to march with in pursuit of Saladin. He arranged this force in five divisions, and placed each under the [Pg 235] command of a competent general. There were two very celebrated bodies of knights that occupied positions of honor in this march. They were the Knights Templars and the Knights of St. John, or Hospitalers, the order that has been described in a previous chapter of this volume. The Templars led the van of the army, and the Hospitalers brought up the rear. The march was commenced on the twenty-second of August, which was not far from two months from the time that Acre was surrendered.

Jaffa.

The course which the army was to take was at first to follow the sea-shore toward the southward to Jaffa, a port nearly opposite to Jerusalem. It was deemed necessary to take possession of Jaffa before going into the interior; and, besides, by moving on along the coast, the ships and galleys containing the stores for the army could accompany them, and supply them abundantly, from time to time, as they might require. By this course, too, they would be drawing nearer to Jerusalem, though not directly approaching it.

Trumpeters.
The evening proclamation in camp.

The arrangements connected with the march of the army were conducted with great ceremony and parade. The knights wore their costly armor, and were mounted on horses splendidly [Pg 236] equipped and caparisoned. In many cases the horses themselves were protected, like the riders, with an armor of steel. The columns were preceded by trumpeters, who awakened innumerable echoes from the mountains, and from the cliffs of the shore, with their animating and exciting music, and innumerable flags and banners, with the most gorgeous decorations, were waving in the air. When the expedition halted at night, heralds passed through the several camps to the sound of trumpets, and pausing at each one, and giving a signal, all the soldiers in the camp kneeled down upon the ground, when the heralds proclaimed in a loud voice three times, God save the Holy Sepulchre, and all the soldiers said Amen.

The slow march.
Saladin's harassing movements.

The march was commenced on the twenty-second of August, and it was about sixty miles from Acre to Jaffa. Of course, an army of thirty thousand men must move very slowly. There is so much time consumed in breaking up the encampment in the morning, and in forming it again at night, and in giving such a mighty host their rest and food in the middle of the day, and the men, moreover, are so loaded with the arms and ammunition, and with the necessary supplies of food and clothing which [Pg 237] they have to carry, that only a very slow progress can be made. In this case, too, the march was harassed by Saladin, who hovered on the flank of the Crusaders, and followed them all the way, sending down small parties from the mountains to attack and cut off stragglers, and threatening the column at every exposed point, so as to keep them continually on the alert. The necessity of being always ready to form in order of battle to meet the enemy, should he suddenly come upon them, restricted them very much in their motions, and made a great deal of manœuvring necessary, which, of course, greatly increased the fatigue of the soldiers, and very much diminished the speed of their progress.

Richard wished much to bring on a general battle, being confident that he should conquer if he could engage in it on equal terms. But Saladin would not give him an opportunity. He kept the main body of his troops sheltered among the mountains, and only advanced slowly, parallel with the coast, where he could watch and harass the movements of his enemies without coming into any general conflict with them.

The plain of Azotus.
The order of battle.

This state of things continued for about three [Pg 238] weeks, and then at last Richard reached Jaffa. The two armies manœuvred for some time in the vicinity of the town, and, finally, they concentrated their forces in the neighborhood of a plain near the sea-shore, at a place called Azotus, which was some miles beyond Jaffa. Saladin had by this time strengthened himself so much that he was ready for battle. He accordingly marched on to the attack. He directed his

147

assault, in the first instance, on the wing of Richard's army which was formed of the French troops that were under the command of the Duke of Burgundy. They resisted them successfully and drove them back. Richard watched the operation, but for a time took no part in it, except to make feigned advances, from time to time, to threaten the enemy, and to harass them by compelling them to perform numerous fatiguing evolutions. His soldiers, and especially the knights and barons in his army, were very impatient at his delaying so long to take an active and an efficient part in the contest. But at last, when he found that the Saracen troops were wearied, and were beginning to be thrown in a little confusion, he gave the signal for a charge, and rode forward at the head of the troop, mounted on his famous [Pg 239] charger, and flourishing his heavy battle-axe in the air.

The charge of Richard's troops.
To retreat is to be defeated.

The onset was terrible. Richard inspirited his whole troop by his reckless and headlong bravery, and by the terrible energy with which he gave himself to the work of slaughtering all who came in his way. The darts and javelins that were shot by the enemy glanced off from him without inflicting any wound, being turned aside by the steel armor that he wore, while every person that came near enough to him to strike him with any other weapon was felled at once to the ground by a blow from the ponderous battle-axe. The example which Richard thus set was followed by his men, and in a short time the Saracens began every where to give way. When, in the case of such a combat, one side begins to yield, it is all over with them. When they turn to retreat, they, of course, become at once defenseless, and the pursuers press on upon them, killing them without mercy and at their pleasure, and with very little danger of being killed themselves. A man can fight very well while he is pursuing, but scarcely at all when he is pursued.

Saladin, defeated, retires.

It was not long before Saladin's army was flying in all directions, the Crusaders pressing [Pg 240] on upon them every where in their confusion, and cutting them down mercilessly in great numbers. The slaughter was immense. About seven thousand of the Saracen troops were slain. Among them were thirty-two of Saladin's highest and best officers. As soon as the Saracens escaped the immediate danger, when the Crusaders had given over the pursuit, they rallied, and Saladin formed them again into something like order. He then commenced a regular and formal retreat into the interior. He first, however, sent detachments to all the country around to dismantle the towns, to destroy all stores of provisions, and to seize and carry away every thing of value that could be of any use to the conquerors. A broad extent of country, through which Richard would have to march in advancing toward Jerusalem, being thus laid waste, the Saracens withdrew farther into the interior, and there Saladin set himself at work to reorganize his broken army once more, and to prepare for new plans of resistance to the invaders.

Richard at Jaffa again.

Richard withdrew with his army to Jaffa, and, taking possession of the town, he established himself there.

Sickness in the army.
Excuses for delaying the march.

It was now September. The season of the [Pg 241] year was hot and unhealthy; and though the allied army had thus far been victorious, still there was a great deal of sickness in the camp, and the soldiers were much exhausted by the fatigue which they had endured, and by their exposure to the sun. Richard was desirous, notwithstanding this, to take the field again, and advance into the interior, so as to follow up the victory which had been gained over Saladin at Azotus; but his officers, especially those of the French division of the army, under the command of the Duke of Burgundy, thought it not safe to move forward so soon. "It would be better to remain a short time in Jaffa," they said, "to recruit the army, and to prepare for advancing in a more sure and efficient manner.

"Besides," said they, "we need Jaffa for a military post, and it will be best to remain here until we shall have repaired the fortifications, and put the place in a good condition of defense."

Lingering at Jaffa.

But this was only an excuse. What the army really desired was to enjoy repose for a time. They found it much more agreeable to live in ease and indulgence within the walls of a town than to march in the hot sun across so arid a country, loaded down as they were with [Pg 242] heavy armor, and kept constantly in a state of anxious and watchful suspense by the danger of sudden attacks from the enemy.

The judgment of historians.

Richard acceded to the wishes of the officers, and decided to remain for a time in Jaffa. But they, instead of devoting themselves energetically to making good again the fortifications of the town, went very languidly to the work. They allowed themselves and the men to spend their time in inaction and indulgence. In the mean time, Saladin had gathered his forces together again, and was drawing fresh recruits every day to his standard from the interior of the country. He was preparing for more vigorous resistance than ever. Richard has been strongly condemned for thus remaining inactive in Jaffa after the battle of Azotus. Historians, narrating the account of his campaign, say that he ought to have marched at once toward Jerusalem before Saladin should have had time to organize any new means of resistance. But it is impossible for those who are at a distance from the scene of action in such a case, and who have only that partial and imperfect account of the facts which can be obtained through the testimony of others, to form any reliable judgment on such a question. Whether it [Pg 243] would be prudent or imprudent for a commander to advance after a battle can be known, in general, only to those who are on the ground, and who have personal knowledge of all the circumstances of the case.

Richard's incursions from Jaffa.
Reconnoitring and foraging.

While Richard remained in Jaffa, he made frequent excursions into the surrounding territory at the head of a small troop of adventurous men who liked to accompany him. Other small detachments were often sent out. These parties went sometimes to collect forage, and sometimes to reconnoitre the country with a view of ascertaining Saladin's position and plans. Richard took great delight in these excursions, nor were they attended with any great danger. At the present day, going out on reconnoitring parties is very dangerous service indeed, for men wear no armor, and they are liable at any moment to be cut down by a Miniè rifle-ball, fired from an unseen hand a mile away. In those days the case was very different. There were no missiles that could be thrown for a greater distance than a few yards, and for all such the heavy steel armor that the knights wore furnished, in general, an ample protection. The only serious danger to be feared was that of coming unwarily upon a superior party of [Pg 244] the enemy lying in ambush to entrap the reconnoitrers, and in being surrounded by them. But Richard had so much confidence in the power of his horse and in his own prodigious personal strength that he had very little fear. So he scoured the country in every direction, at the head of a small attendant squadron, whenever he pleased, considering such an excursion in the light of nothing more than an exciting morning ride.

Richard's predatory excursions.
Sir William's stratagem.
Sir William's ransom.

Of course, after going out many times on such excursions and coming back safely, men gradually become less cautious, and expose themselves to greater and greater risks. It was so with Richard and his troop, and several times they ventured so far as to put themselves in very serious peril. Indeed, Richard once or twice very narrowly escaped being taken prisoner. At one time he was saved by the generosity of one of his knights, named Sir William. The king and his party were surprised by a large party of Saracens, and nearly surrounded. For a moment it was uncertain whether they would be able to effect their retreat. In the midst of the fray, Sir William called out that he was the king, and this so far divided the attention of the party as to confuse them somewhat, [Pg 245] and break the force and concentration of their attack, and thus Richard succeeded in making his escape. Sir William, however, was taken prisoner and carried to Saladin, but he was immediately liberated by Richard's paying the ransom that Saladin demanded for him.

Incident of the Knights Templars.

At another time word came to him suddenly in the town that a troop of Knights Templars were attacked and nearly surrounded by Saracens, and that, unless they had help immediately, they would be all cut off. Richard immediately seized his armor and began to put it on, and at the same time he ordered one of his earls to mount his horse and hurry out to the rescue of the Templars with all the horsemen that were ready, saying also that he would follow himself, with more men, as soon as he could put his armor on. Now the armoring of a knight for battle in the Middle Ages was as long an operation as it is at the present day for a lady to dress for a ball. The several pieces of which the armor was composed were so heavy, and so complicated, moreover, in their fastenings, that they could only be put on by means of much aid from assistants. While Richard was in the midst of the process, another messenger came, saying that the danger of the Templars was imminent.

[Pg 246]

"Then I must go," said Richard, "as I am. I should be unworthy of the name of king if I were to abandon those whom I have promised to stand by and succor in every danger."

Richard's feats of prowess among the Saracens.

So he leaped upon his horse and rode on alone. On arriving at the spot, he plunged into the thickest of the fight, and there he fought so furiously, and made such havoc among the Saracens with his battle-axe, that they fell back, and the Templars, and also the party that had gone out with the earl, were rescued, and made good their retreat to the town, leaving only on the field those who had fallen before Richard arrived.

The Troubadours.

Many such adventures as this are recorded in the old histories of this campaign, and they were made the subjects of a great number of songs and ballads, written and sung by the Troubadours in those days in honor of the valiant deeds of the Crusaders.

Negotiations for peace.

The armies remained in Jaffa through the whole of the month of September. During this time a sort of negotiation was opened between Richard and Saladin, with a view to agreeing, if possible, upon some terms of peace. The object, on the part of Saladin, in these negotiations, was probably delay, for the longer he could [Pg

247] continue to keep Richard in Jaffa, the stronger he would himself become, and the more able to resist Richard's intended march to Jerusalem. Richard consented to open these negotiations, not knowing but that some terms might possibly be agreed upon by which Saladin would consent to restore Jerusalem to the Christians, and thus end the war.

Saphadin.

The messenger whom Saladin employed in these negotiations was Saphadin, his brother. Saphadin, being provided with a safe-conduct for this purpose, passed back and forth between Jaffa and Saladin's camp, carrying the propositions and counter-propositions to and fro. Saphadin was a very courteous and gentlemanly man, and also a very brave soldier, and Richard formed quite a strong friendship for him.

A marriage proposed.
King Richard offered his sister in marriage to Saphadin.

A number of different plans were proposed in the course of the negotiation, but there seemed to arise insuperable objections against them all. At one time, either at this period or subsequently, when Richard returned again to the coast, a project was formed to settle the dispute, as quarrels and wars were often settled in those days, by a marriage. The plan was for Saladin and Richard to cease their hostility to each other, and become friends and allies; the consideration [Pg 248] for terminating the war being, on Richard's side, that he would give his sister Joanna, the ex-queen of Sicily, in marriage to Saphadin; and that Saladin, on his part, should relinquish Jerusalem to Richard. Whether it was that Joanna would not consent to be thus conveyed in a bargain to an Arab chieftain as a part of a price paid for a peace, or whether Saladin did not consider her majesty as a full equivalent for the surrender of Jerusalem, the plan fell through like all the others that had been proposed, and at length the negotiations were fully abandoned, and Richard began again to prepare for taking the field.

[Pg 249]

Chapter XVI.

Reverses.

Feuds in the Christian army.

By this time very serious dissensions and difficulties had arisen in the army of the Crusaders. There were a great many chieftains who felt very independent of each other, and feuds and quarrels of long standing broke out anew, and with more violence than ever. There were many different opinions, too, in respect to the course which it was now best to pursue. Richard, however, contrived yet to maintain some sort of authority, and he finally decided to commence his march from Jaffa.

The march in November.

It was now November. The fall rains began to set in. The distance to Jerusalem was but about thirty-two miles. The army advanced to Ramula, which is about fifteen miles from Jaffa, but they endured very great hardships and sufferings from the extreme inclemency of the season. The soldiers were wet to the skin by drenching rains. Their provisions were soaked and spoiled, and their armor was rusted, and much of it rendered useless. When they [Pg 250] attempted to pitch their tents at night at Ramula, the wind tore them from their fastenings, and blew the canvas away, so as to deprive them of shelter.

The army weakened by disease, mutiny, and desertion.

Of course, these disasters increased the discontent in the army, and, by making the men impatient and ill-natured, increased the bitterness of their quarrels. The army finally advanced, however, as far as Bethany, with a forlorn hope of being strong enough, when they should arrive there, to attack Jerusalem; but this hope, when the time came, Richard was obliged to abandon. The rain and exposure had brought a great deal of disease into the camp. The men were dying in great numbers. This mortality was increased by famine, for the stores which the army had brought with them were spoiled by the rain, and Saladin had so laid waste the country that no fresh supplies could be obtained. Then, in addition to this, the soldiers, finding their sufferings intolerable, and seeing no hope of relief, began to desert in great numbers, and Richard finally found that there was no alternative for him but to fall back again to the sea-shore.

The return to Ascalon.

Instead of going to Jaffa, however, he proceeded to Ascalon. Ascalon was a larger and [Pg 251] stronger city than Jaffa. At least it had been stronger, and its fortifications were more extensive, though the place had been dismantled by Saladin before he left the coast. This town, as you will see by the map, is situated toward the southern part of Palestine, near to the confines of Egypt, and it had been a place of importance as a sort of entrepôt of commerce between Egypt and the Holy Land. Richard began to think that it would be necessary for him to establish his army somewhat permanently in the strong places on the coast, and wait until he could obtain re-enforcements from Europe before attempting again to advance toward Jerusalem. He thought it important, therefore, to take possession of Ascalon, and thus — Acre and Jaffa being already strongly garrisoned — the whole coast would be secure under his control.

Rebuilding the fortifications.

Accordingly, on his retreat from Jerusalem, he proceeded with a large portion of his army to Ascalon, and immediately commenced the work of repairing the walls and rebuilding the towers, not knowing how soon Saladin might be upon him.

Saladin presses upon the retiring army.
Skirmishing.

Indeed, Saladin and his troops had followed Richard's army on their retreat from Bethany, [Pg 252] and had pressed them very closely all the way. It was at one time quite doubtful whether they would succeed in making good their retreat to Ascalon. The Saracen horsemen hovered in great numbers on the rear of Richard's army, and made incessant skirmishing attacks upon them. Richard placed a strong body of the Knights of St. John there to keep them off. These knights were well armed, and they were brave and well-trained warriors. They beat back the Saracens whenever they came near. Still, many of the knights were killed, and straggling parties, from time to time, were cut off, and the whole army was kept in a constant state of suspense and excitement, during the whole march, by the continual danger of an attack. When, at length, they approached the sea-shore, and turned to the south on the way to Ascalon, they were a little more safe, for the sea defended them on one side. Still, the Saracens turned with them, and hovered about their left flank, which was the one that was turned toward the land, and harassed the march all the way. The progress of the troops was greatly retarded too, as well as made more fatiguing, by the presence of such an enemy; for they were not only obliged to move more slowly [Pg 253] when they were advancing, but they could only halt at night in places which were naturally strong and easily to be defended, for fear of an assault upon their encampment in the night. During the night, too, notwithstanding all the precautions they could take to secure a strong and safe position, the men were continually roused from their slumbers by an alarm that the Saracens were coming upon them, when they would rush from their tents, and seize their arms, and prepare for a combat; and then, after a time, they would learn that the expected attack was only a feint made by a small body of the enemy just to harass them.

Contrivances of the enemy to harass the army.

It might seem, at first view, that such a warfare as this would weary and exhaust the pursuers as much as the pursued, but in reality it is not so. In the case of a night alarm, for instance, the whole camp of the Crusaders would be aroused from their sleep by it, and kept in a state of suspense for an hour or more before the truth could be fully ascertained, while to give the alarm would require only a very small party from the army of the Saracens, the main body retiring as usual to sleep, and sleeping all night undisturbed.

At length Richard reached Ascalon in safety, [Pg 254] and posted himself within the walls, while Saladin established his camp at a safe distance in the interior of the country. Of course, the first thing which he found was to be done, as has already been remarked, was to repair and strengthen the walls, and it was evident that no time was to be lost in accomplishing this work.

Difficulties which the king met with in repairing Ascalon.

But, unfortunately, the character of the materials of which Richard's army was composed was not such as to favor any special efficiency in conducting an engineering operation. All the knights, and a large proportion of the common soldiers, deemed themselves gentlemen. They had volunteered to join the crusade from high and romantic notions of chivalry and religion. They were perfectly ready, at any time, to fight the Saracens, and to kill or be killed, whichever fate the fortune of war might assign them; but to bear burdens, to mix mortar, and to build walls, were occupations far beneath them; and the only way to induce them to take hold of this work seems to have been for the knights and officers to set them the example.

The troops unwilling to labor.

Thus, in repairing the walls of Acre, all the highest officers of the army, with Richard himself at the head of them, took hold of the work with their own hands, and built away on the [Pg 255] walls and towers like so many masons. Of course, the body of the soldiery had no excuse for declining the work, when even the king did not consider himself demeaned by it, and the whole army joined in making the reparations with great zeal.

Resentment of Leopold.

But such kind of zeal as this is not often very enduring. The men had accomplished this work very well at Acre, but now, in undertaking a second operation of the kind, their ardor was found to be somewhat subsided. Besides, they were discouraged and disheartened in some degree by the results of the fruitless campaign they had made into the interior, and worn down by the fatigues they had endured on their march. Still, the knights and nobles generally followed Richard's example, and worked upon the walls to encourage the soldiery. One, however, absolutely refused; this was Leopold, the Archduke of Austria, whose flag Richard had pulled down from one of the towers in Acre, and trampled upon as it lay on the ground. The archduke had never forgiven this insult.

The present which Richard made to Berengaria.

Indeed, this rudeness on the part of Richard was not a solitary instance of his enmity. It was only a new step taken in an old quarrel. Richard and the duke had been on very ill [Pg 256] terms before. The reader will perhaps recollect that when Richard was at Cyprus he made captive a young princess, the daughter of the king, and that he made a present of her, as a handmaid and companion, to Queen Berengaria. Berengaria and Joanna, when they left Cyprus, brought the young princess with them, and when they were established with the king in the palace at Acre, she remained with them. She was treated kindly, it is true, and was made a member of the family, but still she was a prisoner. Such captives were greatly prized in those days as presents for ladies of high rank, who kept them as pets, just as they would, at the present day, a beautiful Canary bird or a favorite pony. They often made intimate and familiar companions of them, and dressed them with great elegance, and surrounded them with every luxury. Still, notwithstanding this gilding of their chains, the poor captives usually pined away their lives in sorrow, mourning continually to be restored to their father and mother, and to their own proper home.

Intercession of Leopold.
Richard's exasperation.

Now it happened that the Archduke of Austria was a relative, by marriage, of the King of Cyprus, and the princess was his niece; consequently, when she arrived at the camp before [Pg 257] Acre as a captive in the hands of the queen, as might naturally have been expected, he took a great interest in her case. He wished to have her released and restored to her father, and he interceded with Richard in her behalf. But Richard would not release her. He was not willing to take her away from Berengaria. The archduke was angry with the king for this refusal, and a quarrel ensued; and it was partly in consequence of this quarrel, or, rather, of the exasperation of mind that was produced by it, that Richard would not allow the archduke's banner to float from the towers of Acre when the city fell into their hands.

Richard expels Leopold from Ascalon.

The archduke felt very keenly the indignity which Richard thus offered him, and though at the time he had no power to revenge it, he remembered it, and remained long in a gloomy and resentful frame of mind. And now, while Richard was endeavoring to encourage and stimulate the soldiers to work on the walls, by inducing the knights and barons to join him in setting the example, Leopold refused. He said that he was neither the son of a carpenter nor of a mason, that he should go to work like a laborer to build walls. Richard was enraged at this answer, and, as the story goes, flew at [Pg 258] Leopold in his passion, and struck and kicked him. He also immediately turned the archduke and all his vassals out of the town, declaring that they should not share the protection of walls that they would not help to build; so they were obliged to encamp without, in company with that portion of the army that could not be accommodated within the walls.

The work goes on.

But, notwithstanding the bad example set thus by the archduke, far the greater portion of the knights, and barons, and high officers of the army joined very heartily in the work of building the walls. Even the bishops, and abbots, and other monks, as well as the military nobles, took hold of the work with great zeal, and the repairs went on much more rapidly than could have been expected. During all this time the army kept their communications open with the other towns along the coast — with Jaffa, and Acre, and other strongholds, so that at length the whole shore was well fortified, and secure in their possession.

Waiting for re-enforcements.
The Abbot of Clairvaux.

Saladin, during all this time, had distributed his troops in various encampments along the line parallel with the coast, and at some distance from it, and for some weeks the two armies remained, in a great degree, quiet in their [Pg 259] several positions. The Crusaders were too much diminished in numbers by the privations and the sickness which they had undergone, as well as by the losses they had suffered in battle, and too much weakened by their internal dissensions, to go out of their strongholds to attack Saladin, while, on the other hand, they were too well protected by the walls of the towns to which they had retreated for Saladin to attack them. Both sides were waiting for re-enforcements. Saladin was indeed continually receiving accessions to his army from the interior, and Richard was expecting them from Europe. He sent to a distinguished ecclesiastic, named the Abbot of Clairvaux, who had a high reputation in Europe, and enjoyed great influence at many of the principal courts. In his letter to the abbot, he requested him to visit the different courts, and urge upon the princes and the people of the different countries the necessity that they should come to the rescue of the Christian cause in the Holy Land. Unless they were willing, he said, that all hope of regaining possession of the Holy Land should be abandoned, they must come with large re-enforcements, and that, too, without any delay.

The truce.
Courtesy of enemies when not at contest.

During the period of delay occasioned by [Pg 260] these circumstances, there was a sort of truce established between the two armies, and the knights on each side mingled together frequently on very friendly terms. Indeed, it was the pride and glory of soldiers in this chivalrous age to treat each other, when not in actual conflict, in a very polite and courteous manner, as if they were not animated by any personal resentment against their enemies, but only by a spirit of fidelity to the prince who commanded them, or to the cause in which they were engaged. Accordingly, when, for any reason, the war was for a time suspended, the combatants became immediately the best friends in the world, and actually vied with each other to see which should evince the most generous courtesy toward their opponents.

Presents.
Saladin's present to Richard.

On the present occasion they often made visits to each other, and they arranged tournaments and other military celebrations which were attended by the knights and chieftains on both sides. Richard and Saladin often sent each other handsome presents. At one time when Richard was sick, Saladin sent him a quantity of delicious fruit from Damascus. The Damascus gardens have been renowned in every age for the peaches, pears, figs, and other fruits [Pg 261] which they produce, and especially for a peculiar plum, famous through all the East. Saladin sent a supply of this fruit to Richard when he heard that he was sick, and accompanied his present with very earnest and, perhaps, very sincere inquiries in respect to the condition of the patient, and expressions of his wishes for his recovery.

The Christian army discouraged.

The disposition of the two commanders to live on friendly terms with each other at this time was increased by the hope which Richard entertained that he might, by some possibility, come to an amicable agreement with Saladin in respect to Jerusalem, and thus bring the war to an end. He was beginning to be thoroughly discontented with his situation, and with every thing pertaining to the war. Nothing since the first capture of Acre had really gone well. His army had been repulsed in its attempt to advance into the interior, and was now hemmed in by the enemy on every side, and shut up in a few towns on the sea-coast. The men under his command had been greatly diminished in numbers, and, though sheltered from the enemy, the force that remained was gradually wasting away from the effects of exposure to the climate and from fatigue. There was no prospect of [Pg 262] any immediate re-enforcements arriving from Europe, and no hope, without them, of being able to take the field successfully against Saladin.

King Richard uneasy respecting the state of England.

Besides all this, Richard was very uneasy in respect to the state of affairs in his own dominions, in England and in Normandy. He distrusted the promises that Philip had made, and was very anxious lest he might, when he arrived in France, take advantage of Richard's absence, and, under some pretext or other, invade some of his provinces. From England he was continually receiving very unfavorable tidings. His mother Eleanora, to whom he had committed some general oversight of his interests during his absence, was beginning to write him alarming letters in respect to certain intrigues which were going on in England, and which threatened to deprive him of his English kingdom altogether. She urged him to return as soon as possible. Richard was exceedingly anxious to comply with this recommendation, but he could not abandon his army in the condition in which it then was, nor could he honorably withdraw it without having previously come to some agreement with Saladin by which the Holy Sepulchre could be secured to the possession of the Christians.

[Pg 263]

Selfishness, not generosity, was the secret motive.

This being the state of the case, he had every motive for pressing the negotiations, and for cultivating, while they were in progress, the most friendly relations possible with Saladin, and for persevering in pressing them as long as the least possible hope remained. Accordingly, during all this time Richard treated Saladin with the greatest courtesy. He sent him many presents, and paid him many polite attentions. All this display of urbanity toward each other, on the part of these ferocious and bloodthirsty men, has been actually attributed by mankind to the instinctive nobleness and generosity of the spirit of chivalry; but, in reality, as is indeed too often the case with the pretended nobleness and generosity of rude and violent men, a cunning and far-seeing selfishness lay at the bottom of it.

Saladin's reason for retaining Jerusalem.

In the course of these negotiations, Richard declared to Saladin that all which the Christians desired was the possession of Jerusalem and the restoration of the true cross, and he said that surely some terms could be devised on which Saladin could concede those two points. But Saladin replied that Jerusalem was as sacred a place in the eyes of Mussulmans, and as dear to them, as it was to the Christians, and [Pg 264] that they could on no account give it up. In respect to the true cross, the Christians, he said, if they could obtain it, would worship it in an idolatrous manner, as they did their other relics; and as the law of the Prophet in the Koran forbade idolatry, they could not conscientiously give it up. "By so doing," said he, "we should be accessories to the sin."

A political marriage.

It was in consequence of the insuperable objections which arose against an absolute surrender of Jerusalem to the Christians that the negotiations took the turn which led to the proposal of a marriage between the ex-Queen Joanna and Saphadin; for, when Richard found that no treaty was possible that would give him full possession of Jerusalem, and the letters which he received from England made more and more urgent the necessity that he should return, he conceived the plan of a sort of joint occupancy of the Holy City by Mussulmans and Christians together. This was to be effected by means of the proposed marriage. The marriage was to be the token and pledge of a surrendering, on both sides, of the bitter fanaticism which had hitherto animated them, and of their determination henceforth to live in peace, notwithstanding their religious differences. If this [Pg 265] state of feeling could be once established, there would be no difficulty, it was thought, in arranging some sort of mixed government for Jerusalem that would secure access to the holy places by both Mussulmans and Christians, and accomplish the ends of the war to the satisfaction of all.

The compromise was opposed by the priests.

It was said that Richard proposed this plan, and that both Saladin and Saphadin evinced a willingness to accede to it, but that it was defeated by the influence of the priests on both sides. The imams among the Mussulmans, and the bishops and monks in Richard's army, were equally shocked at this plan of making a "compromise of principle," as they considered it, and forming a compact between evil and good. The men of each party devoutly believed that the cause which their side espoused was the cause of God, and that that of the other was the cause of Satan, and neither could tolerate for a moment any proposal for a union, or an alliance of any kind, between elements so utterly antagonistical. And it was in vain, as both commanders knew full well, to attempt to carry such an arrangement into effect against the conviction of the priests; for they had, on both sides, so great an influence over the masses of the [Pg 266] people that, without their approval, or at least their acquiescence, nothing could be done.

The scheme of joint occupancy of Jerusalem abandoned.

So the plan of an alliance and union between the Christians and the Mohammedans, with a view to a joint occupancy and guardianship of the holy places in Jerusalem was finally abandoned, and Joanna gave up the hope, or was released from the fear, as the case may have been, of having a Saracen for a husband.

[Pg 267]

Chapter XVII.

The old Man of the Mountains.

1191

The conquest of Jerusalem by Godfrey of Bouillon.
History of the contest for the title of King of Jerusalem.

One of the greatest sources of trouble and difficulty which Richard experienced in managing his heterogeneous mass of followers was the quarrel which has been already alluded to between the two knights who claimed the right to be the King of Jerusalem, whenever possession of that city should by any means be obtained. The reader will recollect, perhaps, that it has already been stated that a very renowned Crusader, named Godfrey of Bouillon, had penetrated, about a hundred years before this time, into the interior of the Holy Land, at the head of a large army, and there had taken possession of Jerusalem; that the earls, and barons, and other prominent knights in his army had chosen him king of the city, and fixed the crown and the royal title upon him and his descendants forever; that when Jerusalem was itself, after a time, lost, the title still remained in Godfrey's family, and that it descended [Pg 268] to a princess named Sibylla; that a knight named Guy of Lusignan married Sibylla, and then claimed the title of King of Jerusalem in the right of his wife; that, in process of time, Sibylla died, and then one party claimed that the rights of her husband, Guy of Lusignan, ceased, since he held them only through his wife, and that thenceforward the title and the crown vested in Isabella, her sister, who was the next heir; that Isabella, however, was married to a man who was too feeble and timid to assert his claims; that, consequently, a more bold and unscrupulous knight, named Conrad of Montferrat, seized her and carried her off, and afterward procured a divorce for her from her former husband, and married her himself; and that then a great quarrel arose between Guy of Lusignan, the husband of Sibylla, and Conrad of Montferrat, the husband of Isabella. This quarrel had now been raging a long time, and all attempts to settle it or to compromise it had proved wholly unavailing.

A delicate question.

The ground which Guy and his friends and adherents took was, that while they admitted that Guy held the title of King of Jerusalem in the right of his wife, and that his wife was now dead, still, being once invested with the crown, [Pg 269] it was his for life, and he could not justly be deprived of it. After his death it might descend very properly to the next heir, but during his lifetime it vested in him.

Conrad, on the other hand, and the friends and adherents who espoused his cause, argued that, since Guy had no claim whatever except what came in and through his wife, of course, when his wife died, his possession ought to terminate. If Sibylla had had children, the crown would have descended to one of them; but she being without direct heirs, it passed, of right, to Isabella, her sister, and that Isabella's husband was entitled to claim and take possession of it in her name.

The Crusaders' motives.

It is obvious that this was a very nice and delicate question, and it would have been a very difficult one for a company of gay and reckless soldiers like the Crusaders to settle if they had attempted to look at it simply as a question of law and right; but the Crusaders seldom troubled themselves with examining legal arguments, and still less with seeking for and applying principles of justice and right in taking sides in the contests that arose among them. The question for each man to consider in such cases was simply, "Which side is it most for my interests [Pg 270] and those of my party that we should espouse? We will take that;" or, "Which side are my rivals and enemies, or those of their party, going to take? We will take the other."

How Richard and Philip took sides in the quarrel.

It was by such considerations as these that the different princes, and nobles, and orders of knights in the army decided how they would range themselves on this great question. As has already been explained, Richard took up the cause of Guy, who claimed through the deceased Sibylla. He had been induced to do so, not by any convictions which he had formed in respect to the merits of the case, but because Guy had come to him while he was in Cyprus, and had made such proposals there in respect to a conjunction with him that Richard deemed it for his interest to accept them. In a similar way, Conrad had waited upon Philip as soon as he arrived before Acre, and had induced him to espouse his, Conrad's, side. If there were two orders of knights in the army, or two bodies of soldiery, that were at ill-will with each other through rivalry, or jealousy, or former quarrels, they would always separate on this question of the King of Jerusalem; and just as certainly as one of them showed a disposition to take the side of Guy, the other would immediately go [Pg 271] over to that of Conrad, and then these old and half-smothered contentions would break out anew.

Thus this difficulty was not only a serious quarrel itself, but it was the means of reviving and giving new force and intensity to a vast number of other quarrels.

The reason of the importance of the quarrel.

It may seem strange that a question like this, which related, as it would appear, to only an empty title, should have been deemed so important; but, in reality, there was something more than the mere title at issue. Although, for the time being, the Christians were excluded from Jerusalem, they were all continually hoping to be very soon restored to the possession of it, and then the king of the city would become a very important personage, not only in his own estimation and in that of the army of Crusaders, but in that of all Christendom. No one knew but that in a few months Jerusalem might come into their hands, either by being retaken through force of arms, or by being ceded in some way through Richard's negotiations with Saladin; and, of course, the greater the probability was that this event would happen, the more important the issue of the quarrel became, and the more angry with each other, and [Pg 272] excited, were the parties to it. Thus Richard found that all his plans for getting possession of Jerusalem were grievously impeded by these dissensions; for the nearer he came, at any time, to the realization of his hopes, the more completely were his efforts to secure the end paralyzed by the increased violence and bitterness of the quarrel that reigned among his followers.

The French maintain Conrad's cause.

The principal supporters of the cause of Conrad were the French, and they formed so numerous and powerful a portion of the army, and they had, withal, so great an influence over other bodies of troops from different parts of Europe, that Richard could not successfully resist them and maintain Guy's claims, and he finally concluded to give up, or to pretend to give up, the contest.

Richard's bargain with Guy.

So he made an arrangement with Guy to relinquish his claims on condition of his receiving the kingdom of Cyprus instead, the unhappy Isaac, the true king of that island, shut up in the Syrian dungeon to which Richard had consigned him, being in no condition to resist this disposition of his dominions. Richard then agreed that Conrad should be acknowledged as King of Jerusalem, and, to seal and settle the [Pg 273] question, it was determined that he should be crowned forthwith.

Richard's reasons for acceding to Conrad's cause.

It was supposed at the time that one reason which induced Richard to give up Guy and adopt Conrad as the future sovereign of the Holy City was, that Conrad was a far more able warrior, and a more influential and powerful man than Guy, and altogether a more suitable person to be left in command of the army in case of Richard's return to England, provided, in the mean time, Jerusalem should be taken; and, moreover, he was much more likely to succeed as a leader of the troops in a march against the city in case Richard were to leave before the conquest should be effected. It turned out, however, in the end, as will be seen in the sequel, that the views with which Richard adopted this plan were of a very different character.

The coronation of Conrad.

Conrad was already the King of Tyre. The position which he thus held was, in fact, one of the elements of his power and influence among the Crusaders. It was determined that his coronation as King of Jerusalem should take place at Tyre, and, accordingly, as soon as the arrangement of the question had been fully and finally agreed upon, all parties proceeded to Tyre, and there commenced at once the preparations [Pg 274] for a magnificent coronation. All the principal chieftains and dignitaries of the army that could be spared from the other posts along the coast went to Tyre to be present at the coronation, the whole army, with the exception of a few malcontents, being filled with joy and satisfaction that the question which had so long distracted their councils and paralyzed their efforts was now at length finally disposed of.

His assassination.
The Hassassins.
The Old Man of the Mountains and his followers.

These bright prospects were all, however, suddenly blighted and destroyed by an unexpected event, which struck every one with consternation, and put all things back into a worse condition than before. As Conrad was passing along the streets of Tyre one day, two men rushed upon him, and with small daggers, which they plunged into his side, slew him. They were so sudden in their movement that all was over before any one could come to Conrad's rescue, but the men who committed the deed were seized and put to the torture. They belonged to a tribe of Arabs called Hassassins. [F] This appellation was taken from the Arabic name of the dagger, which was the only armor that they wore. Of course, with such a weapon as this, [Pg 275] they could do nothing effectual in a regular battle with their enemies. Nor was this their plan. They never came out and met their enemies in battle. They lived among the mountains in a place by themselves, under the command of a famous chieftain, whom they called the *Ancient*, and sometimes the *Lord of the Mountains*. The Christians called him the *Old Man of the Mountains*, and under this name he and his band of followers acquired great fame.

The reckless spirit of the Hassassins.

They were, in fact, not much more than a regularly-organized band of robbers and murderers. The men were extremely wily and adroit; they could adopt any disguise, and penetrate without suspicion wherever they chose to go. They were trained, too, to obey, in the most unhesitating and implicit manner, any orders whatever that the chieftain gave them. Sometimes they were sent out to rob; sometimes to murder an individual enemy, who had, in some way or other, excited the anger of the chief. Thus, if any leader of an armed force attempted to attack them, or if any officer of government adopted any measures to bring them to justice, they would not openly resist, but would fly to their dens and fastnesses, and [Pg 276] conceal themselves there, and then soon afterward the chieftain would send out his emissaries, dressed in a suitable disguise, and with their little *hassassins* under their robes, to watch an opportunity and kill the offender. It is true they were usually, in such cases, at once seized, and were often put to death with horrible tortures; but so great was their enthusiasm in the cause of their chief, and so high the exaltation of spirit to which the point of honor carried them, that they feared nothing, and were never known to shrink from the discharge of what they deemed their duty.

Seizure of the murderers.

The stabs which the two Hassassins gave to Conrad were so effectual that he fell dead upon the spot. The people that were near rushed to his assistance, and while some gathered round the bleeding body, and endeavored to stanch the wounds, others seized the murderers and bore them off to the castle. They would have pulled them to pieces by the way if they had not desired to reserve them for the torture.

The torture as a means of eliciting evidence.
Conflicting accounts.

The torture is, of course, in every respect, a wretched way of eliciting evidence. So far as it is efficacious at all in eliciting declarations, it tends to lead the sufferer, in thinking what he shall say, to consider, not what is the truth, [Pg 277] but what is most likely to satisfy his tormentors and make them release him. Accordingly, men under torture say any thing which they suppose their questioners wish to hear. At one moment it is one thing, and the next it is another, and the men who conduct the examination can usually report from it any result they please.

Uncertainty respecting the motive of Conrad's murder.

A story gained great credit in the army, and especially among the French portion of it, immediately after the examination of these men, that they said that they had been hired by Richard himself to kill Conrad, and this story produced every where the greatest excitement and indignation. On the other hand, the friends of Richard declared that the Hassassins had stated that they were sent by their chieftain, the Old Man of the Mountain, and that the cause was a quarrel that had long been standing between Conrad and him. It is true that there had been such a quarrel, and, consequently, that the Old Man would be, doubtless, very willing that Conrad should be killed. Indeed, it is probable that, if Richard was really the original instigator of the murder, he would have made the arrangement for it with the Old Man, and not directly with the subordinates. It was, in fact, a part of the regular and settled business [Pg 278] of this tribe to commit murders for pay. The chieftain might have the more readily undertaken this case from having already a quarrel of his own with Conrad on hand. It was never fully ascertained what the true state of the case was. The Arab historians maintain that it was Richard's work. The English writers, on the contrary, throw the blame on the Old Man. The English writers maintain, moreover, that the deed was one which such a man as Richard was very little likely to perform. He was, it is true, they say, a very rude and violent man—daring, reckless, and often unjust, and even cruel—but he was not treacherous. What he did, he did in the open day; and he was wholly incapable of such a deed as pretending deceitfully that he would accede to Conrad's claims with a view of throwing him off his guard, and then putting him to death by means of hired murderers.

False and spurious honor.

This reasoning will seem satisfactory to us or otherwise, according to the views we like to entertain in respect to the genuineness of the sense of generosity and honor which is so much boasted of as a characteristic of the spirit of chivalry. Some persons place great reliance upon it, and think that so gallant and courageous [Pg 279] a knight as Richard must have been incapable of any such deed as a secret assassination. Others place very little reliance upon it. They think that the generosity and nobleness of mind to which this class of men make such great pretension is chiefly a matter of outside show and parade, and that, when it serves their purpose, they are generally ready to resort to any covert and dishonest means which will help them to accomplish their ends, however truly dishonorable such means may be, provided they can conceal their agency in them. For my part, I am strongly inclined to the latter opinion, and to believe that there is nothing in the human heart that we can really rely upon in respect to human conduct and character but sound and consistent moral principle.

General opinion of Richard's conduct.

At any rate, it is unfortunate for Richard's cause that among those who were around him at the time, and who knew his character best, the prevailing opinion was against him. It was generally believed in the army that he was really the secret author of Conrad's death. The event produced a prodigious excitement throughout the camp. When the news reached Europe, it awakened a very general indignation there, especially among those who were inclined [Pg 280] to be hostile to Richard. Philip, the King of France, professed to be alarmed for his own safety. "He has employed murderers to kill Conrad, my friend and ally," said he, "and the next thing will be that he will send some of the Old Man of the Mountain's emissaries to thrust their daggers into me."

Suspicions of Philip.

So he organized an extra guard to watch at the gates of his palace, and to attend him whenever he went out, and gave them special instructions to watch against the approach of any suspicious strangers. The Emperor of Germany too, and the Archduke of Austria, whom Richard had before made his enemies, were filled with rage and resentment against him, the effects of which he subsequently felt very severely.

The events consequent on Conrad's death.
Appearance of Count Henry.
He becomes king of Jerusalem.

In the mean time, the excitement in the camp immediately on the death of Conrad became very strong, and it led to serious disturbances. The French troops rose in arms and attempted to seize Tyre. Isabella, Conrad's wife, in whose name Conrad had held the title to the crown of Jerusalem, fled to the citadel, and fortified herself there with such troops as adhered to her. The camp was in confusion, and there was imminent danger that the two parties into which [Pg 281] the army was divided would come to open war. At this juncture, a certain nephew of Richard's, Count Henry of Champagne, made his appearance. He persuaded the people of Tyre to put him in command of the town; and supported as he was by Richard's influence, and by the acquiescence of Isabella, he succeeded in restoring something like order. Immediately afterward he proposed to Isabella that she should marry him. She accepted his proposal, and so he became King of Jerusalem in her name.

The French party, and those who had taken the side of Conrad in the former quarrel, were greatly exasperated, but as the case now stood they were helpless. They had always maintained that Isabella was the true sovereign, and it was through her right to the succession, after Sibylla's death, that they had claimed the crown for Conrad; and now, since Conrad was dead, and Isabella had married Count Henry, they could not, with any consistency, deny that the new husband was fully entitled to succeed the old. They might resent the murder of Conrad as much as they pleased, but it was evident that nothing would bring him back to life, and nothing could prevent Count Henry being now universally regarded as the King of Jerusalem.

[Pg 282]

The question at rest.

So, after venting for a time a great many loud but fruitless complaints, the aggrieved parties allowed their resentment to subside, and all acquiesced in acknowledging Henry as King of Jerusalem.

Dissatisfaction.
The king's proclamation.

Besides these difficulties, a great deal of uneasiness and discontent arose from rumors that Richard was intending to abandon Palestine, and return to Normandy and England, thus leaving the army without any responsible head. The troops knew very well that whatever semblance of authority and subordination then existed was due to the presence of Richard, whose high rank and personal qualities as a warrior gave him great power over his followers, not-withstanding their many causes of complaint against him. They knew, too, that his departure would be the signal of universal disorder, and would lead to the total dissolution of the army. The complaints and the clamor which arose from this cause became so great in all the different towns and fortresses along the coast, that, to appease them, Richard issued a proclamation stating that he had no intention of leaving the army, but that it was his fixed purpose to remain in Palestine at least another year.

[Pg 283]

Chapter XVIII.

The Battle of Jaffa.

1192
The battle of Jaffa.

W hen, at last, the state of Richard's affairs had been reduced, by the causes mentioned in the last chapter, to a very low
ebb, he suddenly succeeded in greatly improving them by a battle.
This battle is known in history as the battle of Jaffa. It was fought in
the early part of the summer of 1192.

Richard gives the army employment.

As soon as he had issued his proclamation declaring to his soldiers that he would positively remain in Palestine for a year, he
began to make preparations for another campaign. The best way, he
thought, to prevent the army from wasting away its energies in
internal conflicts between the different divisions of it was to give
those energies employment against the common enemy; so he put
every thing in motion for a new march into the interior. He left garrisons in the cities of the coast, sufficient, as he judged, to protect
them from any force which the Saracens were likely to send against
them in his absence, and forming the remainder in order of [Pg 284]
march, he set out from his head-quarters at Jaffa, and began to advance once more toward Jerusalem.

Uncomfortable news from England.
Richard's resolution.

Of course, this movement revived, in some degree, the spirit of
his army, and awakened in them new hopes. Still, Richard himself
was extremely uneasy, and his mind was filled with solicitude and
anxiety. Messengers were continually coming from Europe with
intelligence which was growing more and more alarming at every
arrival. His brother John, they said, in England, was forming

schemes to take possession of the kingdom in his own name. In France, Philip was invading his Norman provinces, and was evidently preparing for still greater aggression. He must return soon, his mother wrote him, or he would lose all. Of course, he was in a great rage at what he called the treachery of Philip and John, and burned to get back and make them feel his vengeance. But he was so tied up with the embarrassments and difficulties that he was surrounded with in the Holy Land, that he thought it absolutely necessary to make a desperate effort to strike at least one decisive blow before he could possibly leave his army, and it was in this desperate state of mind that he set out upon his march. It was near the end of May.

[Pg 285]

Account of the country through which the army marched.

The army advanced for several days. They met with not much direct opposition from the Saracens, for Saladin had withdrawn to Jerusalem, and was employed in strengthening the fortifications there, and making every thing ready for Richard's approach. But the difficulties which they encountered from other causes, and the sufferings of the army in consequence of them, were terrible. The country was dry and barren, and the weather hot and unhealthy. The soldiers fell sick in great numbers, and those that were well suffered extremely from thirst and other privations incident to a march of many days through such a country in such a season. There were no trees or shelter of any kind to protect them from the scorching rays of the sun, and scarcely any water to be found to quench their thirst. The streams were very few, and all the wells that could be found were soon drunk dry. Then there was great difficulty in respect to provisions. A sufficient supply for so many thousands could not be brought up from the coast, and all that the country itself had produced—which was, in fact, very little—was carried away by the Saracens as Richard advanced. Thus the army found itself environed with great difficulties, and before [Pg 286] many days it was reduced to a condition of actual distress.

The approach to Jerusalem.
Hebron.

The expedition succeeded, however, in advancing to the immediate vicinity of Jerusalem. Early in June they encamped at Hebron, which is about six miles from Jerusalem, toward the south. Here they halted; and Richard remained here some days, weighed down with perplexity and distress, and extremely harassed in mind, being wholly unable to decide what was best to be done.

The prize in sight.

From a hill in the neighborhood of Hebron Jerusalem was in sight. There lay the prize which he had so long been striving to obtain, all before him, and yet he was utterly powerless to take it. For this he had been manœuvring and planning for years. For this he had exhausted all the resources of his empire, and had put to imminent hazard all the rights and interests of the crown. For this he had left his native land, and had brought on, by a voyage of three thousand miles, all the fleets and armies of his kingdom; and now, with the prize before him, and all Europe looking on to see him grasp it, his hand had become powerless, and he must turn back, and go away as he came.

[Pg 287]

Saladin strongly established in Jerusalem.
Richard's self-reproaches.

Richard saw at once that it must be so; for while, on the one hand, his army was well-nigh exhausted, and was reduced to a state of such privation and distress as to make it nearly helpless, Saladin was established in Jerusalem almost impregnably. While the divisions of Richard's army had been quarreling with each other on the sea-coast, he had been strengthening the walls and other defenses of the city, until they were now more formidable than ever. Richard received information, too, that all the wells and cisterns of water around the city had been destroyed by the Saracens, so that, if they were to advance to the walls and commence a siege, they would soon be obliged to raise it, or perish there with thirst. So great was Richard's distress of mind under these circumstances, that it is said, when he was conducted to the hill from which Jerusalem was to be seen, he could not bear to look at it. He held his shield up before his eyes to shut out the sight of it, and said that he was not worthy to look upon the city, since he had shown himself unable to redeem it.

There was a council of war held to consider what it was best to do. It was a council of perplexity and despair. Nobody could tell what [Pg 288] it was best to do. To go back was disgrace. To go forward was destruction; and it was impossible for them to remain where they were.

A new expedient.
The proposed march upon Cairo.

In his desperation Richard conceived of a new plan, that of marching southward and seizing Cairo. The Saracens derived almost all the stores of provisions for the use of their armies from Cairo, and Hebron was on the road to it. The way was open for Richard's army to march in that direction, and, by carrying this plan into execution, they would, at least, get something to eat. Besides, it would be a mode of withdrawing from Jerusalem that would not be quite a retreat. Still, these reasons were wholly insufficient to justify such a measure, and it is not probable that Richard seriously entertained the plan. It is much more likely that he proposed the idea of a march upon Cairo as a means of amusing the minds of his knights and soldiers, and diminishing the extreme disappointment and vexation which they must have felt in relinquishing the plan of an attack upon Jerusalem, and that he intended, after proceeding a short distance on the way toward Egypt, to find some pretext for turning down toward the sea-shore, and re-establishing himself in his cities on the coast.

[Pg 289]

The hopeless condition of the army.

At any rate, whether it was the original plan or not, such was the result. As soon as the encampment was broken up, and the army commenced its march, and the troops learned that the hope of recovering the Holy Sepulchre, and all the other lofty aspirations and desires which had led them so far, and through so many hardships and dangers, were now to be abandoned, they were first enraged, and then they sank into a condition of utter recklessness and despair. All discipline was at an end. No one seemed now to care what became of the expedition or of themselves. The French soldiers, under the Duke of Burgundy, revolted openly, and declared they would go no farther. The troops from Germany joined them. So

Richard gave up the plan, or seemed to give it up, and gave orders to march to Acre; and there, at last, the army arrived in a state of almost utter dissolution.

Saladin at Jaffa.

In a short time the news came to them that Saladin had followed them down, and had seized upon Jaffa. He had taken the town, and shut up the garrison in the citadel, whither they had fled for safety; and tidings came that, unless Richard very soon came to the rescue, the citadel would be compelled to surrender.

[Pg 290]

Richard's measures to succor Jaffa.

Richard immediately ordered that all the troops that were in a condition to march should set out immediately, to proceed down the coast from Acre to Jaffa. He himself, he said, would hasten on by sea, for the wind was fair, and a part of his force, all that he had ships enough in readiness to convey, could go much quicker by water than by land, besides the advantage of being fresh on their arrival for an attack on the enemy. So he assembled as many ships as could be got ready, and embarked a select body of troops on board of them. There were seven of the ships. He took the command of one of them himself. The Duke of Burgundy, with the French troops under his command, refused to go.

His fleet arrives there.

The little fleet set sail immediately and ran down the coast very rapidly. When they came to Jaffa they found that the town was really in possession of the Saracens, and that large bodies of the enemy were assembled on the shore to prevent the landing of Richard's forces. This array appeared so formidable that all the knights and officers on board the ships urged Richard not to attempt to attack them, but to wait until the body of the army should arrive by land.

Landing.

But Richard was desperate and reckless. He declared that he *would* land; and he uttered [Pg 291] an awful imprecation against those who should hesitate to follow him. He brought the boats up as near the shore as possible, and then, with his battle-axe in his right hand, and his shield hung about his neck, so as to have his left hand at liberty, he leaped into the water, calling upon the rest to come on. They all followed his example, and, as soon as they gained the shore, they made a dreadful onset upon the Saracens that were gathered on the beach. The Saracens were driven back. Richard made such havoc among them with his battle-axe, and the men following him were made so resolute and reckless by his example, that the ranks of the enemy were broken through, and they fled in all directions.

The onset upon the Saracens.
Jaffa retaken.

Richard and his men then rushed on to the gates of the town, and almost before the Saracens who were in possession of them could recover from their surprise, the gates were seized, those who had been stationed at them were slain or driven away, and then Richard and his troops, rushing through, closed them, and the Saracens that were within the town were shut in. They were soon all overpowered and slain, and thus the possession of the town was recovered.

[Pg 292]

Both sides awaiting assistance.

But this was not the end, as Richard and his men knew full well. Though they had possession of the town itself, they were surrounded by a great army of Saracens, that were hovering around them on the plain, and rapidly increasing in numbers; for Saladin had sent orders to the interior directing all possible assistance to be sent to him. Richard himself, on the other hand, was hourly expecting the arrival of the main body of his troops by land.

They arrived the next day, and then came on the great contest. Richard's troops, on their arrival, attacked the Saracens from without, while he himself, issuing from the gates, assaulted them from the side next the town. The Crusaders fought with the utmost desperation. They knew very well that it was the crisis of their fate. To lose that battle was to lose all. The Saracens, on the other hand, were not under any such urgent pressure. If overpowered, they could retire again to the mountains, and be as secure as before.

The Saracens defeated.

They *were* overpowered. The battle was fought long and obstinately, but at length Richard was victorious, and the Saracens were driven off the ground.

[Pg 293-4]

SALADIN'S PRESENT.
The story of Saladin's present of horses to his enemy.

Various accounts are given by the different [Pg 295] writers who have narrated the history of this crusade, of a present of a horse made by Saladin to Richard in the course of the war, and the incident has been often commented upon as an evidence of the high and generous sentiments which animated the combatants in this terrible crusade in their personal feelings toward each other. One of the stories makes the case an incident of this battle. The Saracens, flying from the field, came to Saladin, who was watching the contest, and, in conversation with him, they pointed out Richard, who was standing among his knights on a small rising ground.

"Why, he is on foot!" exclaimed Saladin. Richard *was* on foot. His favorite charger, Favelle, was killed under him that morning, and as he had come from Acre in haste and by sea, there was no other horse at hand to supply his place.

Saladin immediately said that that was not as it should be. "The King of England," said he, "should not fight on foot like a common soldier." He immediately sent over to Richard, with a flag of truce, two splendid horses. King Richard accepted the present, and during the remainder of the day he fought on one of the horses which his enemy had thus sent him.

[Pg 296]

The romantic story of the treacherous gift.

One account adds a romantic embellishment to this story by saying that Saladin sent only one horse at first—the one that he supposed most worthy of being sent as a gift from one sovereign to another; but that Richard, before mounting him himself, directed one of his knights to mount him and give him trial. The knight found the horse wholly unmanageable. The animal took the bits between his teeth and galloped furiously back to the camp of Saladin, carrying his rider with him, a helpless prisoner. Saladin was exceedingly chagrined at this result; he was afraid Richard might suppose that he sent him an unruly horse from a treacherous design to do him some injury. He accordingly received the knight who had been borne so unwillingly to his camp in the most courteous manner, and providing another horse for him, he dismissed him with presents. He also sent a second horse to Richard, more beautiful than the first, and one which he caused Richard to be assured that he might rely upon as perfectly well trained.

[Pg 297]

Chapter XIX.

The Truce.

1192

The result of the battle of Jaffa greatly strengthened and improved the condition of the Crusaders, and in the same proportion it weakened and discouraged Saladin and the Saracens. But, after all, instead of giving to either party the predominance, it only placed them more nearly on a footing of equality than before. It began to be pretty plain that neither of the contending parties was strong enough, or would soon be likely to be strong enough to accomplish its purposes. Richard could not take Jerusalem from Saladin, nor could Saladin drive Richard out of the Holy Land.

Richard and Saladin agree upon a three years' truce.

In this state of things, it was finally agreed upon between Richard and Saladin that a truce should be made. The negotiations for this truce were protracted through several weeks, and the summer was gone before it was concluded. It was a truce for a long period, the duration of it being more than three years. Still, it was strictly a truce, not a peace, since a termination was assigned to it.

[Pg 298]

Richard's reason for this course.
The treaty.

Richard preferred to make a truce rather than a peace for the sake of appearances at home. He did not wish that it should be understood that, in leaving the Holy Land and returning home, he abandoned all design of recovering the Holy Sepulchre. He allowed three years, on the supposition that that would be time enough for him to return home, to set every thing in order in his dominions, to organize a new crusade on a larger scale, and to come back again. In the mean time, he reserved, by a stipulation of the treaty, the right to occupy, by such portion of his army as he should leave behind, the portion of territory on the coast which he had conquered, and which he then held, with the exception of one of the cities, which one he was to give up. The terms of the treaty, in detail, were as follows:

STIPULATIONS OF THE TREATY.

The coast.

1. The three great cities of Tyre, Acre, and Jaffa, with all the smaller towns and castles on the coast between them, with the territory adjoining, were to be left in the possession of the Christians, and Saladin bound himself that they should not be attacked or molested in any way there during the continuance of the truce.

[Pg 299]

Ascalon to be dismantled.

2. Ascalon, which lay farther to the south, and was not necessary for the uses of Richard's army, was to be given up; but Saladin was to pay, on receiving it, the estimated cost which Richard had incurred in rebuilding the fortifications. Saladin, however, was not to occupy it himself as a fortified town. It was to be so far dismantled as only to be used as a commercial city.

3. The Christians bound themselves to remain within their territory in peace, to make no excursions from it for warlike purposes into the interior, nor in any manner to injure or oppress the inhabitants of the surrounding country.

Pilgrims to Jerusalem protected.

4. All persons who might desire to go to Jerusalem in a peaceful way as visitors or pilgrims, whether they were knights or soldiers belonging to the army, or actual pilgrims arriving at Acre from the different Christian countries of Europe, were to be allowed to pass freely to and fro, and Saladin bound himself to protect them from all harm.

5. The truce thus agreed upon was to continue in force three years, three months, three weeks, three days, and three hours; and at the end of that time, each party was released from all obligations

arising under the treaty, and either [Pg 300] was at liberty immediately to resume the war.

Events consequent upon the truce.

The signing of the treaty was the signal for general rejoicing in all divisions of the army. One of the first fruits of it was that the knights and soldiers all immediately began to form parties for visiting Jerusalem. It was obvious that all could not go at once; and Richard told the French soldiers who were under the Duke of Burgundy that he did not think they were entitled to go at all. They had done nothing, he said, to help on the war, but every thing to embarrass and impede it, and now he thought that they did not deserve to enjoy any share of the fruits of it.

Visiting the Holy City.
Saladin restraining the Saracens from revenge.

Three large parties were formed and they proceeded, one after the other, to visit the Holy City. There was some difficulty in respect to the first party, and it required all Saladin's authority to protect them from insult or injury by the Saracen people. The animosity and anger which they had been so long cherishing against these invaders of their country had not had time to subside, and many of them were very eager to avenge the wrongs which they had suffered. The friends and relatives of the hostages whom [Pg 301] Richard had massacred at Acre were particularly excited. They came in a body to Saladin's palace, and, falling on their knees before him, begged and implored him to allow them to take their revenge on the inhuman murderers, now that they had them in their power; but Saladin would not listen to them a moment. He refused their prayer in the most absolute and positive manner, and he took very effectual measures for protecting the party of Christians during the whole duration of their visit.

The question being thus settled that the Christian visitors to Jerusalem were to be protected, the excitement among the people gradually subsided; and, indeed, before long, the current of feeling inclined the other way, so that, when the second party arrived, they were received with great kindness. Perhaps the first party had taken care to conduct themselves in such a manner during their visit, and in going and returning, as to conciliate the good-will of their enemies. At any rate, after their visit there was no difficulty, and many in the camp, who had been too distrustful of Saracenic faith to venture with them, now began to join the other parties that were forming, for all had a great curiosity to see the city for the sake of [Pg 302] which they had encountered so many dangers and toils.

The visit of the bishop to Jerusalem.

With the third party a bishop ventured to go. It was far more dangerous for a high dignitary of the Christian Church to join such an expedition than for a knight or a common soldier, both because such a man was a more obnoxious object of Mohammedan fanaticism, and thus more likely, perhaps, to be attacked, and also because, in case of an attack, being unarmed and defenseless, he would be unable to protect himself, and be less able even to act efficiently in making his escape than a military man, who, as such, was accustomed to all sorts of surprises and frays.

The bishop, however, experienced no difficulty. On the contrary, he was received with marks of great distinction. Saladin made special arrangements to do him honor. He invited him to his palace, and there treated him with great respect, and held a long conversation with him. In the course of the conversation Saladin desired to know what was commonly said of him in the Christian camp.

"What is the common opinion in your army," he asked, "in respect to Richard and to me?"

[Pg 303]

He wished to know which was regarded as the greatest hero.

"My king," replied the bishop, "is regarded the first of all men living, both in regard to his valorous deeds and to the generosity of his character. That I can not deny. But your fame also is very exalted among us; and it is the universal opinion in our army that if you were only converted to Christianity, there would not be in the world two such princes as Richard and you."

Saladin's just opinion of King Richard.

In the course of further conversation Saladin admitted that Richard was a great hero, and said that he had a great admiration for him.

"But then," he added, "he does wrong, and acts very unwisely, in exposing himself so recklessly to personal danger, when there is no sufficient end in view to justify it. To act thus evinces rashness and recklessness rather than true courage. For myself, I prefer the reputation of wisdom and prudence rather than that of mere blind and thoughtless daring."

The institution for the entertainment of pilgrims.

The bishop, in his conversation with Saladin, represented to him that it was necessary for the comfort of the pilgrims who should from time to time visit Jerusalem that there should be some public establishment to receive and entertain [Pg 304] them, and he asked the sultan's permission to found such institutions. Saladin acceded to this request, and measures were immediately adopted by the bishop to carry the arrangement into effect.

Richard himself did not visit Jerusalem. The reason he assigned for this was that he was sick at the time. Perhaps the real reason was that he could not endure the humiliation of paying a visit, by the mere permission of an enemy, to the city which he had so long set his heart upon entering triumphantly as a conqueror.

[Pg 305]

Chapter XX.

The Departure from Palestine.

1192

Richard's reasons for returning home.

Ⓞne of the chief objects which Richard had in view in concluding the truce with Saladin was to be able to have an honorable
pretext for leaving the Holy Land and setting out on his return to
England. He had received many letters from his mother urging him
to come, and giving him alarming accounts of the state of things
both in England and Normandy.

Causes of internal dissension in England and Normandy.

In England, the reader will perhaps recollect that Richard, when
he set out on the Crusade, had appointed his brother John regent, in
connection with his mother Eleanora, but that he had also, in order
to raise money, appointed several noblemen of high standing and
influence to offices of responsibility, which they were to exercise, in
a great measure, independent of John. And, not content with ap-
pointing a suitable number of these officers, he multiplied them
unnecessarily, and in some instances conveyed the same jurisdic-
tion, as it were, to different persons, thus virtually selling the same
[Pg 306] office to two different men. Of course, this was not done
openly and avowedly. The transactions were more or less covered
up and concealed under different disguises. For example, after selling the post of chief justiciary, which was an office of great power
and emolument, to one nobleman, and receiving as much money for
it as the nobleman was willing to pay, he afterward appointed other
noblemen as assistant justiciaries, exacting, of course, a large sum of
money from each of them, and granting them, in consideration of it,
much the same powers as he had bestowed upon the chief justiciary. Of course, such a proceeding as this could only result in continual contentions and quarrels among the appointees, to break out

as soon as Richard should be gone. But the king cared little for that, so long as he could get the money.

Longchamp's disguise.
His escape from England.

The quarrels did break out immediately after Richard sailed. There were various parties to them. There were Eleanora and John, each claiming to be the regent. Then there were two powerful noblemen, both maintaining that they had been invested with the supreme power by virtue of the offices which they held. The name of one of them was Longchamp. He contrived to place himself, for a time, quite at the [Pg 307] head of affairs, and the whole country was distracted by the wars which were waged between him and his partisans and the partisans of John. Longchamp was at last defeated, and was obliged to fly from the kingdom in disguise. He was found one day by some fishermen's wives, on the beach near Dover, in the disguise of an old woman, with a roll of cloth under his arm, and a yard-stick in his hand. He was waiting for a boat which was to take him across the Channel into France. He disguised himself in that way that he might not be known, and when seen from behind the metamorphosis was almost complete. The women, however, observed something suspicious in the appearance of the figure, and so contrived to come nearer and get a peep under the bonnet, and there they saw the black beard and whiskers of a man.

Notwithstanding this discovery, Longchamp succeeded in making his escape.

Philip's oath broken.

As to Normandy, Richard's interests were in still greater danger than in England. King Philip had taken the most solemn oaths before he left the Holy Land, by which he bound himself not to molest any of Richard's dominions, or to take any steps hostile to him, while he — that [Pg 308] is, Richard — remained away; and that if he should have any cause of quarrel against him, he would abstain from all attempts to enforce his rights until at least six months after Richard's return. It was only on condition of this agreement that Richard would consent to remain in Palestine in command of the Crusade, and allow Philip to return.

Pretext for invading Normandy.

But, notwithstanding this solemn agreement, and all the oaths by which it was confirmed, no sooner was Philip safe in France than he commenced operations against Richard's dominions. He began to make arrangements for an invasion of some of Richard's territories in Normandy, under pretext of taking possession again of Alice's dower, which it was agreed, by the treaty made at Messina, should be restored to him. But it had also been agreed at that treaty that the time for the restoration of the dowry should be after Richard's return, so that the plans of invasion which Philip was now forming involved clearly a very gross breach of faith, committed without any pretense or justification whatever. This instance, and multitudes of others like it to be found in the histories of those times, show how little there was that was genuine and reliable in the lofty sense [Pg 309] of honor often so highly lauded as one of the characteristics of chivalry.

Proposed marriage of John and Alice.

In justice, however, to all concerned, it must be stated that Philip's knights and nobles remonstrated so earnestly against this breach of faith, that Philip was compelled to give up his plan, and to content himself in his operations against Richard with secret intrigues instead of open war. As he knew that John was endeavoring to supplant Richard in his kingdom, he sent to him and proposed to join him in this plan, and to help him carry it into execution; and he offered him the hand of Alice, the princess whom Richard had discarded, to seal and secure the alliance. John was quite pleased with this proposal; and information of these intrigues, more or less definite, came to Richard in Palestine about the time of the battle of Jaffa, from Eleanora, who contrived in some way to find out what was going on. The tidings threw Richard into a fever of anxiety to leave Palestine and return home.

Richard's return unannounced.

It was about the first of October that Richard set sail from Acre on his return, with a small squadron containing his immediate attendants. He himself embarked in a war-ship. The queens, taking with them the captive princess [Pg 310] of Cyprus and the other members of their family, went as they came, in a vessel specially arranged for them, and under the care of their old protector, Stephen of Turnham. The queens embarked first in their vessel and sailed away. Richard followed soon afterward. His plan was to leave the coast as quietly and in as private a manner as possible. If it were to be understood in France and England that he was on his return, he did not know what plans might be formed to intercept him. So he kept his departure as much as possible a secret, and the more completely to carry out this design, he gave up for the voyage all his royal style and pretensions, and dressed himself as a simple knight.

Sailing from Palestine.
Richard's apostrophe to the Holy Land.

The vessels slipped away from the coast, one after another, in the evening, in a manner to attract as little attention as possible. They made but little progress during the night. In the morning the shore was still in view, though fast disappearing. Richard gazed upon it as he stood on the deck of his galley, and then took leave of it by stretching out his hands and exclaiming,

"Most holy land, farewell! I commend thee to God's keeping and care. May He give [Pg 311] me life and health to return and rescue thee from the hands of the infidel."

The effect of this apostrophe on the by-standers, and on those to whom the by-standers reported it, was excellent, and it was probably for the sake of this effect that Richard uttered it.

[Pg 312]

Chapter XXI.

Richard made Captive.

1192

The returning Crusaders met by a storm.

I t was now late in the season, and the autumnal gales had begun to blow. It was but a very short time after the vessels left the port before so severe a storm came on that the fleet was dispersed, and many of the vessels were driven upon the neighboring coasts and destroyed. The Crusaders that had been left in Acre and Jaffa were rather pleased at this than otherwise. They had been indignant at Richard and the knights who were with him for having left them, to return home, and they said now that the storm was a judgment from Heaven against the men on board the vessels for abandoning their work, and going away from the Holy Land, and leaving the tomb and the cross of Christ unredeemed. Some of the ships, it is said, were thrown on the coasts of Africa, and the seamen and knights, as fast as they escaped to the shore, were seized and made slaves.

Richard's ship, and also the one in which the [Pg 313] queens were embarked, being stronger and better manned than the others, weathered the gale. After it was over, the queens' vessel steered for Sicily, where, in due time, they arrived in safety.

Richard's sudden change of course.

Richard did not intend to trust himself to go to any place where he was known. Accordingly, as soon as he found himself fairly separated from all the other vessels, he suddenly changed his course, and turned northward toward the mouth of the Adriatic Sea. He landed at the island of Corfu. [G] Here he dismissed his ship, and took three small galleys instead, to go up to the head of the Adriatic

Sea, and thence to make his way homeward by land through the heart of Germany.

His route homeward.

He probably thought that this was the safest and best course that he could take. He did not dare to go through France for fear of Philip. To go all the way by sea, which would require him to sail out through the Straits of Gibraltar into the Atlantic, would require altogether too long and dangerous a voyage for so late a season of the year. The only alternative left was to attempt to pass through Germany; and, as the German powers were hostile [Pg 314] to him, it was not safe for him to undertake this unless he went in disguise.

King Richard traveling in disguise of a pilgrim.

So he sailed in the three galleys which he procured in Corfu to the head of the Adriatic Sea, and landed at a place called Zara. Here he put on the dress of a pilgrim. He had suffered his hair and beard to grow long, and this, with the flowing robes of his pilgrim's dress, and the crosier which he bore in his hand, completed his disguise.

But, though he might make himself *look* like a pilgrim, he could not act like one. He was well provided with money, and his mode of spending it, though it might have been, perhaps, very sparing for a king, was very lavish for a pilgrim; and the people, as he passed along, wondered who the party of strangers could be. Partly to account for the comparative ease and comfort with which he traveled, Richard pretended that he was a merchant, and, though making his pilgrimage on foot, was by no means poor.

Richard's enemies in Germany.

Richard knew very well that he was incurring a great risk in attempting to pass through Germany in this way, for the country was full of his foes. The Emperor of Germany was his special enemy, on account of his having supported [Pg 315] Tancred's cause in Sicily, the emperor himself, as the husband of the Lady Constance, having been designated by the former King of Sicily as his successor. Richard's route led, too, through the dominions of the Archduke of Austria, whom he had quarreled with and incensed so bitterly in the Holy Land. Besides this, there were various chieftains in that part of the country, relatives of Conrad of Montferrat, whom every body believed that Richard had caused to be murdered.

Fancied security.

Richard was thus passing through a country full of enemies, and he might naturally be supposed to feel some anxiety about the result; but, instead of proceeding cautiously, and watching against the dangers that beset him, he went on quite at his ease, believing that his good fortune would carry him safely through.

Richard solicits a passport.

He went on for some days, traveling by lonely roads through the mountains, until at length he approached a large town. The governor of the town was a man named Maynard, a near relative of Conrad, and it seems that in some way or other he had learned that Richard was returning to England, and had reason to suppose that he might endeavor to pass that way. Richard did not think it prudent to attempt to [Pg 316] go through the town without a passport, so he sent forward a page whom he had in his party to get one. He gave the page a very valuable ruby ring to present to the governor, directing him to say that it was a present from a pilgrim merchant, who, with a priest and a few other attendants, was traveling through the country, and wished for permission to go through his town.

Maynard's answer.

The governor took the ring, and after examining it attentively and observing its value, he said to the page,

"This is not the present of a pilgrim, but of a prince. Tell your master that I know who he is. He is Richard, King of England. Nevertheless, he may come and go in peace."

The alarm given.

Richard was very much alarmed when the page brought back the message. That very night he procured horses for himself and one or two others, and drove on as fast as he could go, leaving the rest of the party behind. The next day those that were left were all taken prisoners, and the news was noised abroad over the country that King Richard was passing through in disguise, and a large reward was offered by the government for his apprehension. Of course, now every body was on the watch for him.

[Pg 317]

King Richard's flight through Germany.

The king, however, succeeded in avoiding observation and going on some distance farther, until at length, at a certain town where he stopped, he was seen by a knight who had known him in Normandy. The knight at once recognized him, but would not betray him. On the contrary, he concealed him for the night, and provided for him a fresh horse the next day. This horse was a fleet one, so that Richard could gallop away upon him and make his escape, in case of any sudden surprise. Here Richard dismissed all his remaining attendants except his page, and they two set out together.

They traveled three days and three nights, pursuing the most retired roads that they could find, and not entering any house during all that time. The only rest that they got was by halting at lonely places by the road side, in the forests, or among the mountains. In these places Richard would remain concealed, while the boy went to a village, if there was any village near, to buy food. He generally got very little, and sometimes none at all. The horse ate whatever he could find. Thus, at the end of the three days, they were all nearly starved.

Richard concealed near Vienna.
His messenger.

Besides this, they had lost their way, and were now drawing near to the great city of Vienna, [Pg 318] the most dangerous place for Richard to approach in all the land. He was, however, exhausted with hunger and fatigue, and from these and other causes he fell sick, so that he could proceed no farther. So he went into a small village near the town, and sent the boy in to the market to buy something to eat, and also to procure some other comforts which he greatly needed. The people in the town observed the peculiar dress of the boy, and his foreign air, and their attention was still more excited by noticing how plentifully he was supplied with money. They asked him who he was. He said he was the servant of a foreign merchant who was traveling through the country, and who had been taken sick near by.

The people seemed satisfied with this explanation, and so they let the boy go.

Torturing the messenger.

Richard was so exhausted and so sick that he could not travel again immediately, and so he had occasion, in a day or two, to send the boy into town again. This continued for some days, and the curiosity of the people became more and more awakened. At last they observed about the page some articles of dress such as were only worn by attendants upon kings. It is surprising that Richard should [Pg 319] have been so thoughtless as to have allowed him to wear them. But such was his character. The people finally seized the boy, and the authorities ordered him to be whipped to make him tell who he was. The boy bore the pain very heroically, but at length they threatened to put him to the torture, and, among other things, to cut out his tongue, if he did not tell. He was so terrified by this that at last he confessed the truth and told them where they might find the king.

The king a captive.

A band of soldiers was immediately sent to seize him. The story is that Richard, at the time when the soldiers arrived, was in the kitchen turning the spit to roast the dinner. After surrounding the house to prevent the possibility of an escape, the soldiers demanded at the door if King Richard was there. The man answered, "No, not unless the Templar was he who was turning the spit in the kitchen." So the soldiers went in to see. The leader exclaimed, "Yes, that is he: take him!" But Richard seized his sword, and, rushing to a position where he could defend himself, declared to the soldiers that he would not surrender to any but their chief. So the soldiers, deeming it desirable to take him alive, paused until they [Pg 320] could send for the archduke. The archduke had left the Holy Land and returned home some time before. Richard, however, did not probably know that he was passing through his dominions.

When the archduke came, Richard, knowing that resistance would be of no avail, delivered up his sword and became a prisoner.

"You are very fortunate," said Leopold. "In becoming my prisoner, you ought to consider yourself as having fallen into the hands of a deliverer rather than an enemy. If you had been taken by any of Conrad's friends, who are hunting for you every where, you would have been instantly torn to pieces, they are so indignant against you."

The archduke imprisons Richard in Tiernsteign.

When the archduke had thus secured Richard, he sent him, for safe keeping, to a castle in the country belonging to one of his barons, and gave notice to the emperor of what had occurred. The name of the castle in which Richard was confined was Tiernsteign.

As soon as the emperor heard that Richard was taken he was overjoyed. He immediately sent to Leopold, the archduke, and claimed the prisoner as his.

[Pg 321-2]

CASTLE AND TOWN OF TIERNSTEIGN.

"*You* can not rightfully hold him," said he. [Pg 323] "A duke can not presume to imprison a king; that duty belongs to an emperor."

The emperor buys the prisoner.

But the archduke was not willing to give Richard up. A negotiation was, however, opened, and finally he consented to sell his prisoner for a large sum of money. The emperor took him away, and what he did with him for a long time nobody knew.

In the mean while, during the period occupied by the voyage of Richard up the Adriatic, by his long and slow journey by land, and by the time of his imprisonment in Tiernsteign, the winter had passed away, and it was now the spring of 1193.

[Pg 324]

Chapter XXII.

The Return to England.

1193-1199

Conjectures of Richard's friends.
Queen Berengaria in Rome.

During all this time the people of England were patiently waiting for Richard's return, and wondering what had become of him. They knew that he had sailed from Palestine in October, and various were the conjectures as to his fate. Some thought that he had been shipwrecked; others, that he had fallen into the hands of the Moors; but all was uncertainty, for no tidings had been heard of him since he sailed from Acre. Berengaria had arrived safely at Messina, and after remaining there a little time she proceeded on her journey, under the care of Stephen, as far as Rome, very anxious all the time about her husband. Here she stopped, not daring to go any farther. She felt safe in Rome, under the protection of the Pope.

Richard in prison.

The emperor attempted to keep Richard's imprisonment a secret. On removing him from Tiernsteign, he shut him up in one of his own castles on the Danube named Durenstein. Here [Pg 325] the king was closely imprisoned. He did not, however, yield to any depression of spirits in view of his hard fate, but spent his time in composing and singing songs, and in drinking and carousing with the people of the castle. Here he remained during the spring and summer of 1193, and all the world were wondering what had become of him.

He is discovered by Blondel.

At length rumors began gradually to circulate in respect to him among the neighboring countries, and the conduct of the emperor, in seizing and imprisoning him, was very generally condemned.

How the intelligence first reached England is not precisely known. One story is, that a celebrated Troubadour, named Blondel, who had known Richard in Palestine, was traveling through Germany, and in his journey he passed along the road in front of the castle where Richard was confined. As he went he was singing one of his songs. Richard knew the song, and so, when the Troubadour had finished a stanza, he sang the next one through the bars of his prison window. Blondel recognized the voice, and instantly understood that Richard had been made a prisoner. He, however, said nothing, but went on, and immediately took measures to make known in England what he had learned.

[Pg 326]

Another account is, that the emperor himself wrote to Philip, King of France, informing him of the King of England's imprisonment in one of his castles, and that some person betrayed a copy of this letter to Richard's friends in England.

Berengaria's distress at the loss of her husband.

It is said that Berengaria received the first intimation in respect to Richard's fate by seeing a belt of jewels offered for sale in Rome which she knew he had had about his person when he left Acre. She made all the inquiry that she could in respect to the belt, but she could only learn that Richard must be somewhere in Germany. It was a relief to her mind to find that he was alive, but she was greatly distressed to think that he was probably a prisoner, and she implored the Pope to interpose his aid and procure his release. The Pope did interpose. He immediately excommunicated Leopold for having seized Richard and imprisoned him, and he threatened to excommunicate the emperor himself if he did not release him.

The people of England sympathize with Richard.

In the mean time, the tidings in respect to Richard's situation produced a great excitement throughout England. John was glad to hear it, and he hoped most devoutly that his brother would never be released. He immediately began [Pg 327] to take measures, in concert with Philip, to secure the crown to himself. The people, on the other hand, were very indignant against the Emperor of Germany, and every one was eager to take some efficient measures to secure the king's release. A great meeting was called of the barons, the bishops, and all the great officers of the realm, at Oxford, where, when they had assembled, they renewed their oaths of allegiance to their sovereign, and then appointed a delegation, consisting of two abbots, to go and visit the king, and confer with him in respect to what was best to be done. They chose two ecclesiastics for their messengers, thinking that they would be more likely to be allowed to go and come without molestation, than knights or barons, or any other military men.

The abbots proceeded to Germany, and there the first interview which they had with Richard was on the road, as the emperor was taking him to the capital in order to bring him before a great assembly of the empire, called the Diet, for the purpose of trial.

Richard was overjoyed to see his friends. He was, however, very much vexed when he heard from them of the plans which John and Philip were engaged in for dispossessing him [Pg 328] of his kingdom. He said, however, that he had very little fear of any thing that they could do.

"My brother John," said he, "has not courage enough to accomplish any thing. He never will get a kingdom by his valor."

When he arrived at the town where the Diet was to be held, Richard had an interview with the emperor. The emperor had two objects in view in detaining Richard a prisoner. One was to prevent his having it in his power to help Tancred in keeping him, the emperor, out of possession of the kingdom of Sicily, and the other was to obtain, when he should set him at liberty at last, a large sum of money for a ransom. When he told Richard what sum of money he would take, Richard refused the offer, saying that he would die rather than degrade his crown by submitting to such terms, and impoverishing his kingdom in raising the money.

King Richard arraigned before the German Diet.
The six charges against the king.

The emperor then, in order to bring a heavier pressure to bear upon him, arraigned him before a Diet as a criminal. The following were the charges which he brought against him:

1. That he had formed an alliance with Tancred, the usurper of Sicily, and thus made himself a partaker in Tancred's crimes.

[Pg 329] 2. That he had invaded the dominions of Isaac, the Christian king of Cyprus, deposed the king, laid waste his dominions, and plundered his treasures; and, finally, had sent the unhappy king to pine away and die in a Syrian dungeon.

3. That, while in the Holy Land, he had offered repeated and unpardonable insults to the Archduke of Austria, and, through him, to the whole German nation.

4. That he had been the cause of the failure of the Crusade, in consequence of the quarrels which he had excited between himself and the French king by his domineering and violent behavior.

5. That he had employed assassins to murder Conrad of Montferrat.

6. That, finally, he had betrayed the Christian cause by concluding a base truce with Saladin, and leaving Jerusalem in his hands.

It is possible that the motive which led the emperor to make these charges against Richard was not any wish or design to have him convicted and punished, but only to impress him more strongly with a sense of the danger of his situation, with a view of bringing him to consent [Pg 330] to the payment of a ransom. At any rate, the trial resulted in nothing but a negotiation in respect to the amount of ransom-money to be paid.

Finally, a sum was agreed upon. Richard was sent back to his prison, and the abbots returned to England to see what could be done in respect to raising the money.

Richard's ransom to be divided between the emperor and the archduke.

The people of England undertook the task not only with willingness, but with alacrity. The amount required was nearly a million of dollars, which, in those days, was a very large sum even for a kingdom to pay. The amount was to be paid in silver. Two thirds of it was to go to the emperor, and the other third to the archduke, who, when he sold his prisoner to the emperor, had reserved a right to a portion of the ransom-money whenever it should be paid.

As soon as two thirds of the whole amount was paid, Richard was to be released on condition of his giving hostages as security for the remainder.

It took a long time to raise all this money, and various embarrassments were created in the course of the transaction by the emperor's bad faith, for he changed his terms from time to time, demanding more and more as he found [Pg 331] that the interest which the people of England took in the case would bear. At last, however, in February, 1194, about two years after Richard was first imprisoned, a sufficient sum arrived to make up the first payment, and Richard was set free.

Richard finally reaches England.

After meeting with various adventures on his journey home, he arrived on the English coast about the middle of March.

The people of the country were filled with joy at hearing of his return, and they gave him a magnificent reception. One of the German barons who came home with him said, when he saw the enthusiasm of the people, that if the emperor had known how much interested in his fate the people of England were, he would not have let him off with so small a ransom.

Flight of John.

John was, of course, in great terror when he heard that Richard was coming home. He abandoned every thing and fled to Normandy. Richard issued a decree that if he did not come back and give himself up within forty days, his estates should all be confiscated. John was thrown into a state of great perplexity by this, and did not know what to do.

As soon as Richard had arranged his affairs a little in England, he determined to be crowned [Pg 332] again anew, as if his two years of captivity had broken the continuity of his reign. Accordingly, a new coronation was arranged, and it was celebrated, as the first one had been, with the greatest pomp and splendor.

The expedition to Normandy.

After this Richard determined to proceed to Normandy, with a view of there making war upon Philip and punishing him for his treachery. On his landing in Normandy, John came to him in a most abject and submissive manner, and, throwing himself at his feet, begged his forgiveness. Eleanora joined him in the petition. Richard said that, out of regard to his mother's wishes, he would pardon him.

"And I hope," said he, "that I shall as easily forget the injuries he has done me as he will forget my forbearance in pardoning him."

Ill treatment of Berengaria.
Richard's reckless immoralities.

Poor Berengaria was very illy rewarded for the devotion which she had manifested to her husband's interests, and for the efforts she had made to secure his release. She had come home from Rome a short time before her husband arrived, but he, when he came, manifested no interest in rejoining her. Instead of that, he connected himself with a number of wicked associates, both male and female, whom he had known before he went to the Holy Land, and [Pg 333] lived a life of open profligacy with them, leaving Berengaria to pine in neglect, alone and forsaken. She was almost heart-broken to be thus abandoned, and several of the principal ecclesiastics of the kingdom remonstrated very strongly with Richard for this wicked conduct. But these remonstrances were of no avail. Richard abandoned himself more and more to drunkenness and profligacy, until at length his character became truly infamous.

A warning.

One day in 1195, when he was hunting in the forest of Normandy, he was met by a hermit, who boldly expostulated with him on account of the wickedness of his life. The hermit told him that, by the course he was pursuing, he was grievously offending God, and that, unless he stopped short in his course and repented of his sins, he was doomed to be brought very soon to a miserable end by a special judgment from heaven.

Sudden illness.

The king pretended not to pay much attention to this prophecy, but not long afterward he was suddenly seized with a severe illness, and then he became exceedingly alarmed. He sent for all the monks and priests within ten miles around to come to him, and began to confess his sins with apparently very deep compunction [Pg 334] for them, and begged them to pray for God's forgiveness. He promised them solemnly that, if God would spare his life, he would return to Berengaria, and thenceforth be a true and faithful husband to her as long as he lived.

Recovery.

He recovered from his sickness, and he so far kept the vows which he had made as to seek a reconciliation with Berengaria, and to live with her afterward, ostensibly at least, on good terms.

The peasant's discovery of hidden treasures.
Videmar denies the story.

For three years after this Richard was engaged in wars with Philip chiefly on the frontiers between France and Normandy. At last, in the midst of this contest, he suddenly came to his death under circumstances of a remarkable character. He had heard that a peasant in the territory of one of his barons, named Videmar, in plowing in the field, had come upon a trap-door in the ground which covered and concealed the entrance to a cave, and that, on going down into the cave, he had found a number of golden statues, with vases full of diamonds, and other treasures, and that the whole had been taken out and carried to the Castle Chaluz, belonging to Videmar. Richard immediately proceeded to Videmar, and demanded that the treasures should be given up to him as the sovereign. Videmar replied that the rumor which [Pg 335] had been spread was false; that nothing had been found but a pot of old Roman coins, which Richard was welcome to have, if he desired them. Richard replied that he did not believe that story; and that, unless Videmar delivered up the statues and jewels, he would storm the castle. Videmar repeated that he had no statues and jewels, and so Richard brought up his troops and opened the siege.

Richard shot by Bertrand's arrow.

During the siege, a knight named Bertrand de Gordon, standing on the wall, and seeing Richard on the ground below in a position where he thought he could reach him with an arrow, drew his bow and took aim. As he shot it he prayed to God to speed it well. The arrow struck Richard in the shoulder. In trying to draw it out they broke the shaft, thus leaving the barb in the wound. Richard was borne to his tent, and a surgeon was sent for to cut out the barb. This made the wound greater, and in a short time inflammation set in, mortification ensued, and death drew nigh. When he found that all was over with him, and that his end had come, he was overwhelmed with remorse, and he died at length in anguish and despair.

King Richard's reign.

His death took place in the spring of 1199. [Pg 336] He had reigned over England ten years, though not one of these years had he spent in that kingdom.

Berengaria lived afterward for thirty years.

The character of the "lion-hearted."

King Richard the First is known in history as the lion-hearted, and well did he deserve the name. It is characteristic of the lion to be fierce, reckless, and cruel, intent only in pursuing the aims which his own lordly and impetuous appetites and passions demand, without the least regard to any rights of others that he may trample under foot, or to the sufferings that he may inflict on the innocent and helpless. This was Richard's character precisely, and he was proud of it. His glory consisted in his reckless and brutal ferocity. He pretended to be the champion and defender of the cause of Christ, but it is hardly possible to conceive of a character more completely antagonistic than his to the just, gentle, and forgiving spirit which the precepts of Jesus are calculated to form.

THE END.

Footnotes:

[A] History of William the Conqueror.

[B] See page 14.

[C] The ampulla used now for anointing the English sovereigns is in the form of an eagle. It is made of the purest chased gold, and weighs about ten ounces. It is deposited in the Tower of London.

[D] The mark is about three dollars.

[E] *Trenc-le-mer*, literally, *Cut the sea*.

[F] The English word *assassins* comes from the name of these men.

[G] For the situation of this island, see the map on page 164.